REBEL CITIES

REBEL CITIES

From the Right to the City
to the Urban Revolution

David Harvey

VERSO
London • New York

First published by Verso 2012
© David Harvey

1 3 5 7 9 10 8 6 4 2

Verso
UK: 6 Meard Street, London W1F 0EG
US: 20 Jay Street, Suite 1010, Brooklyn, NY 11201
www.versobooks.com

Verso is the imprint of New Left Books

ISBN-13: 978-1-84467-882-2

British Library Cataloguing in Publication Data
A catalogue record for this book is available from the British Library

Library of Congress Cataloging-in-Publication Data
Harvey, David, 1935–
Rebel cities : from the right to the city to the urban revolution / David Harvey.
   p. cm.
Includes bibliographical references and index.
ISBN 978-1-84467-882-2 (alk. paper) -- ISBN 978-1-84467-904-1
1. Anti-globalization movement--Case studies. 2. Social justice--Case studies.
3. Capitalism--Case studies. I. Title.
HN17.5.H355 2012
303.3'72--dc23

2011047924

Typeset in Minion by MJ Gavan, Cornwall
Printed in the US by Maple Vail

For Delfina
and all other graduating students everywhere

Contents

Henri Lefebvre's Vision

Sometime in the mid 1970s in Paris I came across a poster put out by the Ecologistes, a radical neighborhood action movement dedicated to creating a more ecologically sensitive mode of city living, depicting an alternative vision for the city. It was a wonderful ludic portrait of old Paris reanimated by a neighborhood life, with flowers on balconies, squares full of people and children, small stores and workshops open to the world, cafés galore, fountains flowing, people relishing the river bank, community gardens here and there (maybe I have invented that in my memory), evident time to enjoy conversations or smoke a pipe (a habit not at that time demonized, as I found to my cost when I went to an Ecologiste neighborhood meeting in a densely smoke-filled room). I loved that poster, but over the years it became so tattered and torn that I had, to my great regret, to throw it out. I wish I had it back! Somebody should reprint it.

The contrast with the new Paris that was emerging and threatening to engulf the old was dramatic. The tall building "giants" around the Place d'Italie were threatening to invade the old city and clasp the hand of that awful Tour Montparnasse. The proposed expressway down the Left Bank, the soulless high-rise public housing (HLMs) out in the 13th arrondissement and in the suburbs, the monopolized commodification on the streets, the plain disintegration of what had once been a vibrant neighborhood life built around artisanal labor in small workshops in the

Marais, the crumbling buildings of Belleville, the fantastic architecture of the Place des Vosges falling into the streets. I found another cartoon (by Batellier). It showed a combine harvester crushing and gobbling up all the old neighborhoods of Paris, leaving high-rise HLMs all in a neat row in its wake. I used it as key illustration in *The Condition of Postmodernity*.

Paris from the early 1960s on was plainly in the midst of an existential crisis. The old could not last, but the new seemed just too awful, soulless and empty to contemplate. Jean-Luc Godard's 1967 film, *Deux ou trois choses que je sais d'elle*, captures the sensibility of the moment beautifully. It depicts married mothers engaging in a daily routine of prostitution, as much out of boredom as of financial need, against the background of an invasion of American corporate capital into Paris, the war in Vietnam (once a very French affair but by then taken over by the Americans), a construction boom of highways and high-rises, and the arrival of a mindless consumerism in the streets and stores of the city. However, Godard's philosophical take—a kind of quizzical, wistful, Wittgensteinian precursor to postmodernism, in which nothing at the center of either the self or society could possibly hold—was not for me.

It was also in this very same year, 1967, that Henri Lefebvre wrote his seminal essay on *The Right to the City*. That right, he asserted, was both a cry and a demand. The cry was a response to the existential pain of a withering crisis of everyday life in the city. The demand was really a command to look that crisis clearly in the eye and to create an alternative urban life that is less alienated, more meaningful and playful but, as always with Lefebvre, conflictual and dialectical, open to becoming, to encounters (both fearful and pleasurable), and to the perpetual pursuit of unknowable novelty.[1]

We academics are quite expert at reconstructing the genealogy of ideas. So we can take Lefebvre's writings of this period and excavate a bit of Heidegger here, Nietzsche there, Fourier somewhere else, tacit critiques of Althusser and Foucault, and, of course, the inevitable framing given by Marx. The fact that this essay was written for the centennial celebrations of the publication of Volume 1 of *Capital* bears mentioning because it has some political significance, as we shall see. But what we academics so often forget is the role played by the sensibility that arises out of the streets around us, the inevitable feelings of loss provoked by the demolitions, what happens when whole quarters (like Les Halles) get re-engineered or *grands ensembles* erupt seemingly out of nowhere, coupled with the exhilaration or annoyance of street demonstrations about this or that, the hopes that lurk as immigrant groups bring life back into a neighborhood (those great Vietnamese restaurants in the 13th arrondissement in the midst of the HLMs), or the despair that flows from the glum desperation of marginalization, police repressions and idle youth lost in the sheer boredom of increasing unemployment and neglect in the soulless suburbs that eventually become sites of roiling unrest.

Lefebvre was, I am sure, deeply sensitive to all of that—and not merely because of his evident earlier fascination with the Situationists and their theoretical attachments to the idea of a psychogeography of the city, the experience of the urban dérive through Paris, and exposure to the spectacle. Just walking out of the door of his apartment in the Rue Rambuteau was surely enough to set all his senses tingling. For this reason I think it highly significant that *The Right to the City* was written before *The Irruption* (as Lefebvre later called it) of May 1968. His essay depicts a situation in which such an irruption was not only possible but almost inevitable (and Lefebvre played his own small part at Nanterre in making it so). Yet the urban roots of that '68 movement remain a much neglected theme in subsequent accounts of that event. I suspect that the urban social movements then existing—the Ecologistes for example—melded into that revolt and helped shape its political and cultural demands in intricate if subterranean ways. And I also suspect, though I have no proof at all, that the cultural transformations in urban life that subsequently occurred, as naked capital masked itself in commodity fetishism, niche marketing, and urban cultural consumerism, played a far from innocent role in the post-'68 pacification (for instance, the newspaper *Libération*, which was founded by Jean-Paul Sartre and others, gradually shifted from the mid '70s to become culturally radical and individualistic but politically lukewarm, if not antagonistic to serious left and collectivist politics).

I make these points because if, as has happened over the last decade, the idea of the right to the city has undergone a certain revival, then it is not to the intellectual legacy of Lefebvre that we must turn for an explanation (important though that legacy may be). What has been happening in the streets, among the urban social movements, is far more important. And as a great dialectician and immanent critic of urban daily life, surely Lefebvre would agree. The fact, for example, that the strange collision between neoliberalization and democratization in Brazil in the 1990s produced clauses in the Brazilian Constitution of 2001 that guarantee the right to the city has to be attributed to the power and significance of urban social movements, particularly around housing, in promoting democratization. The fact that this constitutional moment helped con-solidate and promote an active sense of "insurgent citizenship" (as James Holston calls it) has nothing to do with Lefebvre's legacy, but everything to do with ongoing struggles over who gets to shape the qualities of daily urban life.[2] And the fact that something like "participatory budgeting," in which ordinary city residents directly take part in allocating portions of municipal budgets through a democratic decision-making process, has been so inspirational has everything to do with many people seeking some kind of response to a brutally neoliberalizing international capital-ism that has been intensifying its assault on the qualities of daily life since the early 1990s. No surprise either that this model developed in Porto Alegre, Brazil—the central place for the World Social Forum.

When all manner of social movements came together at the US Social Forum in Atlanta in June 2007, to take another example, and decided to form a national Right to the City Alliance (with active chapters in cities such as New York and Los Angeles), in part inspired by what the urban social movements in Brazil had accomplished, they did so without for the most part knowing Lefebvre's name. They had individually concluded after years of struggling on their own particular issues (homelessness, gentrification and displacement, criminalization of the poor and the different, and so on) that the struggle over the city as a whole framed their own particular struggles. Together they thought they might more readily make a difference. And if various movements of an analogous kind can be found elsewhere, it is not simply out of some fealty to Lefebvre's ideas but precisely because Lefebvre's ideas, like theirs, have primarily arisen out of the streets and neighborhoods of ailing cities. Thus in a recent compilation, right to the city movements (though of diverse orientation) are reported as active in dozens of cities around the world.[3]

So let us agree: the idea of the right to the city does not arise primarily out of various intellectual fascinations and fads (though there are plenty of those around, as we know). It primarily rises up from the streets, out from the neighborhoods, as a cry for help and sustenance by oppressed peoples in desperate times. How, then, do academics and intellectuals (both organic and traditional, as Gramsci would put it) respond to that cry and that demand? It is here that a study of how Lefebvre responded is helpful—not because his responses provide blueprints (our situation is very different from that of the 1960s, and the streets of Mumbai, Los Angeles, São Paulo and Johannesburg are very different from those of Paris), but because his dialectical method of immanent critical inquiry can provide an inspirational model for how we might respond to that cry and demand.

Lefebvre understood very well, particularly after his study of *The Paris Commune*, published in 1965 (a work inspired to some degree by the Situationists' theses on the topic), that revolutionary movements frequently if not always assume an urban dimension. This immediately put him at odds with the Communist Party, which held that the factory-based proletariat was the vanguard force for revolutionary change. In commemorating the centennial of the publication of Marx's *Capital* with a tract on *The Right to the City*, Lefebvre was certainly intending a provocation to conventional Marxist thinking, which had never accorded the urban much significance in revolutionary strategy, even though it mythologized the Paris Commune as a central event in its history.

In invoking the "working class" as the agent of revolutionary change throughout his text, Lefebvre was tacitly suggesting that the revolutionary working class was constituted out of urban rather than exclusively factory workers. This, he later observed, is a very different kind of class formation—fragmented and divided, multiple in its aims and needs, more often itinerant, disorganized and fluid rather than solidly implanted. This is a thesis with which I have always been in accord (even before I read Lefebvre), and subsequent work in urban sociology (most notably by one of Lefebvre's erstwhile but errant students, Manuel Castells) amplified that idea. But it is still the case that much of the traditional left has had trouble grappling with the revolutionary potential of urban social movements. They are often dismissed as simply reformist attempts to deal with specific (rather than systemic) issues, and therefore as neither revolutionary nor authentically class movements.

There is, therefore, a certain continuity between Lefebvre's situational polemic and the work of those of us who now seek to address the right to the city from a revolutionary as opposed to reformist perspective. If anything, the logic behind Lefebvre's position has intensified in our own times. In much of the advanced capitalist world the factories have either disappeared or been so diminished as to decimate the classical industrial working class. The important and ever-expanding labor of making and sustaining urban life is increasingly done by insecure, often part-time and disorganized low-paid labor. The so-called "precariat" has displaced the traditional "proletariat." If there is to be any revolutionary movement in our times, at least in our part of the world (as opposed to industrializing China), the problematic and disorganized "precariat" must be reckoned with. How such disparate groups may become self-organized into a revolutionary force is the big political problem. And part of the task is to understand the origins and nature of their cries and demands.

I am not sure how Lefebvre would have responded to the Ecologistes' poster vision. Like me, he would probably have smiled at its ludic vision, but his theses on the city, from *The Right to the City* to his book on *La Révolution Urbaine* (1970), suggest that he would have been critical of its nostalgia for an urbanism that had never been. For it was Lefebvre's central conclusion that the city we had once known and imagined was fast disappearing and that it could not be reconstituted. I would agree with this, but assert it even more emphatically, because Lefebvre takes very little care to depict the dismal conditions of life for the masses in some of his favored cities of the past (those of the Italian Renaissance in Tuscany). Nor does he dwell on the fact that in 1945 most Parisians lived without indoor plumbing in execrable housing conditions (where they froze in winter and baked in summer) in crumbling neighborhoods, and that something had to be, and—at least during the 1960s—was being done to remedy that. The problem was that it was bureaucratically organized and implemented by a French dirigiste state without a whiff of democratic input or an ounce of playful imagination, and that it merely etched relations of class privilege and domination into the very physical landscape of the city.

Lefebvre also saw that the relation between the urban and the rural—or as the British like to call it, between the country and the city—was being radically transformed, that the traditional peasantry was disappearing and that the rural was being urbanized, albeit in a way that offered a new consumerist approach to the relation to nature (from weekends and leisure in the countryside to leafy, sprawling suburbs) and a capitalist, productivist approach to the supply of agricultural commodities to urban markets, as opposed to self-sustaining peasant agriculture. Furthermore, he presciently saw that this process was "going global," and that under such conditions the question of the right to the city (construed as a distinctive thing or definable object) had to give way to some vaguer question of the right to urban life, which later morphed in his thinking into the more general question of the right to *The Production of Space* (1974).

The fading of the urban–rural divide has proceeded at a differential pace throughout the world, but there is no question that it has taken the direction that Lefebvre predicted. The recent pell-mell urbanization of China is a case in point, with the percentage of the population residing in rural areas decreasing from 74 percent in 1990 to about 50 percent in 2010, and the population of Chongqing increasing by 30 million over the past half-century. Though there are plenty of residual spaces in the global economy where the process is far from complete, the mass of humanity is thus increasingly being absorbed within the ferments and cross-currents of urbanized life.

This poses a problem: to claim the right to the city is, in effect, to claim a right to something that no longer exists (if it ever truly did). Furthermore, the right to the city is an empty signifier. Everything depends on who gets to fill it with meaning. The financiers and developers can claim it, and have every right to do so. But then so can the homeless and the *sans-papiers*. We inevitably have to confront the question of whose rights are being identified, while recognizing, as Marx puts it in *Capital*, that "between equal rights force decides." The definition of the right is itself an object of struggle, and that struggle has to proceed concomitantly with the struggle to materialize it.

The traditional city has been killed by rampant capitalist development, a victim of the never-ending need to dispose of overaccumulating capital driving towards endless and sprawling urban growth no matter what the social, environmental, or political consequences. Our political task, Lefebvre suggests, is to imagine and reconstitute a totally different kind of city out of the disgusting mess of a globalizing, urbanizing capital run amok. But that cannot occur without the creation of a vigorous anti-capitalist movement that focuses on the transformation of daily urban life as its goal.

As Lefebvre knew full well from the history of the Paris Commune, socialism, communism, or for that matter anarchism in one city is an impossible proposition. It is simply too easy for the forces of bourgeois reaction to surround the city, cut its supply lines and starve it out, if not invade it and slaughter all who resist (as happened in Paris in 1871). But that does not mean we have to turn our backs upon the urban as an incu-bator of revolutionary ideas, ideals, and movements. Only when politics focuses on the production and reproduction of urban life as the central labor process out of which revolutionary impulses arise will it be possi-ble to mobilize anti-capitalist struggles capable of radically transforming daily life. Only when it is understood that those who build and sustain urban life have a primary claim to that which they have produced, and that one of their claims is to the unalienated right to make a city more after their own heart's desire, will we arrive at a politics of the urban that will make sense. "The city may be dead," Lefebvre seems to say, but "long live the city!"

So is pursuit of the right to the city the pursuit of a chimera? In purely physical terms this is certainly so. But political struggles are animated by visions as much as by practicalities. Member groups within the Right to the City Alliance consist of low-income tenants in communities of color fighting for the kind of development that meets their desires and needs; homeless people organizing for their right to housing and basic services; and LGBTQ youth of color working for their right to safe public spaces. In the collective political platform they designed for New York, the coali-tion sought a clearer and broader definition of that public that not only can truly access so-called public space, but can also be empowered to create new common spaces for socialization and political action. The term "city" has an iconic and symbolic history that is deeply embedded in the pursuit of political meanings. The city of God, the city on a hill, the relationship between city and citizenship—the city as an object of utopian desire, as a distinctive place of belonging within a perpetually shifting spatio-temporal order—all give it a political meaning that mobilizes a crucial political imaginary. But Lefebvre's point, and here he is certainly in league with if not indebted to the Situationists, is that there are already multiple practices within the urban that themselves are full to overflowing with alternative possibilities.

Lefebvre's concept of heterotopia (radically different from that of Foucault) delineates liminal social spaces of possibility where "something different" is not only possible, but foundational for the defining of revolutionary trajectories. This "something different" does not necessarily arise out of a conscious plan, but more simply out of what people do, feel, sense, and come to articulate as they seek meaning in their daily lives. Such practices create heterotopic spaces all over the place. We do not have to wait upon the grand revolution to constitute such spaces. Lefebvre's theory of a revolutionary movement is the other way round: the spontaneous coming together in a moment of "irruption," when disparate heterotopic groups suddenly see, if only for a fleeting moment, the possibilities of collective action to create something radically different.

That coming together is symbolized by Lefebvre in the quest for centrality. The traditional centrality of the city has been destroyed. But there is an impulse towards and longing for its restoration which arises again and again to produce far-reaching political effects, as we have recently seen in the central squares of Cairo, Madrid, Athens, Barcelona, and even Madison, Wisconsin and now Zuccotti Park in New York City. How else and where else can we come together to articulate our collective cries and demands?

It is at this point, however, that the urban revolutionary romanticism that so many now attribute to and love about Lefebvre crashes against the rock of his understanding of capitalist realities and capital's power. Any spontaneous alternative visionary moment is fleeting; if it is not seized at the flood, it will surely pass (as Lefebvre witnessed firsthand in the streets of Paris in '68). The same is true of the heterotopic spaces of difference that provide the seed-bed for revolutionary movement. In *The Urban Revolution* he kept the idea of heterotopia (urban practices) in tension with (rather than as an alternative to) isotopy (the accomplished and rationalized spatial order of capitalism and the state), as well as with utopia as expressive desire. "The isotopy-heterotopy difference," he argued, "can only be understood dynamically ... Anomic groups construct heterotopic spaces, which are eventually reclaimed by the dominant praxis."

Lefebvre was far too well aware of the strength and power of the dominant practices not to recognize that the ultimate task is to eradicate those practices through a much broader revolutionary movement. The whole capitalist system of perpetual accumulation, along with its associated structures of exploitative class and state power, has to be overthrown and replaced. Claiming the right to the city is a way-station on the road to that goal. It can never be an end in itself, even if it increasingly looks to be one of the most propitious paths to take.

Section I:
The Right to the City

CHAPTER ONE

The Right to the City

We live in an era when ideals of human rights have moved center-stage both politically and ethically. A lot of political energy is put into promoting, protecting, and articulating their significance in the construction of a better world. For the most part the concepts circulating are individualistic and property-based and, as such, do nothing to challenge hegemonic liberal and neoliberal market logics, or neoliberal modes of legality and state action. We live in a world, after all, where the rights of private property and the profit rate trump all other notions of rights one can think of. But there are occasions when the ideal of human rights takes a collective turn, as when the rights of workers, women, gays, and minorities come to the fore (a legacy of the long-standing labor movement and, for example, the 1960s Civil Rights movement in the United States, which was collective and had a global resonance). Such struggles for collective rights have, on occasion, yielded important results.

Here I want to explore another kind of collective right—that to the city in the context of a revival of interest in Henri Lefebvre's ideas on the topic, and the emergence of all sorts of social movements around the world that are now demanding such a right. How, then, can this right be defined?

The city, the noted urban sociologist Robert Park once wrote, is "man's most consistent and on the whole, his most successful attempt to remake the world he lives in more after his heart's desire. But, if the city is the world which man created, it is the world in which he is henceforth condemned to live. Thus, indirectly, and without any clear sense of the nature of his task, in making the city man has remade himself."[1] If Park is correct, then the question of what kind of city we want cannot be divorced from the question of what kind of people we want to be, what kinds of social relations we seek, what relations to nature we cherish, what style of life we desire, what aesthetic values we hold. The right to the city is, therefore, far more than a right of individual or group access to the resources that the city embodies: it is a right to change and reinvent the city more after our hearts' desire. It is, moreover, a collective rather than an individual right, since reinventing the city inevitably depends upon the exercise of a collective power over the processes of urbanization. The freedom to make and remake ourselves and our cities is, I want to argue, one of the most precious yet most neglected of our human rights. How best then to exercise that right?

Since, as Park avers, we have hitherto lacked any clear sense of the nature of our task, it is useful first to reflect on how we have been made and remade throughout history by an urban process impelled onwards by powerful social forces. The astonishing pace and scale of urbanization over the last hundred years means, for example, that we have been remade several times over without knowing why or how. Has this dramatic urbanization contributed to human well-being? Has it made us into better people, or left us dangling in a world of anomie and alienation, anger and frustration? Have we become mere monads tossed around in an urban sea? These were the sorts of questions that preoccupied all manner of nineteenth-century commentators, such as Friedrich Engels and Georg Simmel, who offered perceptive critiques of the urban personas then emerging in response to rapid urbanization.[2] These days it is not hard to enumerate all manner of urban discontents and anxieties, as well as excitements, in the midst of even more rapid urban transformations. Yet we somehow seem to lack the stomach for systematic critique. The maelstrom of change overwhelms us even as obvious questions loom. What, for example, are we to make of the immense concentrations of wealth, privilege, and consumerism in almost all the cities of the world in the midst of what even the United Nations depicts as an exploding "planet of slums"?[3]

To claim the right to the city in the sense I mean it here is to claim some kind of shaping power over the processes of urbanization, over the ways in which our cities are made and remade, and to do so in a fundamental and radical way. From their very inception, cities have arisen through the geographical and social concentration of a surplus product. Urbanization has always been, therefore, a class phenomenon of some sort, since surpluses have been extracted from somewhere and from somebody, while control over the use of the surplus typically lies in the hands of a few (such as a religious oligarchy, or a warrior poet with imperial ambitions). This general situation persists under capitalism, of course, but in this case there is a rather different dynamic at work. Capitalism rests, as Marx tells us, upon the perpetual search for surplus value (profit). But to produce surplus value capitalists have to produce a surplus product. This means that capitalism is perpetually producing the surplus product that urbanization requires. The reverse relation also holds. Capitalism needs urbanization to absorb the surplus products it perpetually produces. In this way an inner connection emerges between the development of capitalism and urbanization. Hardly surprisingly, therefore, the logistical curves of growth of capitalist output over time are broadly paralleled by the logistical curves of urbanization of the world's population.

Let us look more closely at what capitalists do. They begin the day with a certain amount of money and end the day with more of it (as profit). The next day they have to decide what to do with the surplus money they gained the day before. They face a Faustian dilemma: reinvest to get even more money or consume their surplus away in pleasures. The coercive laws of competition force them to reinvest, because if one does not reinvest then another surely will. For a capitalist to remain a capitalist, some surplus must be reinvested to make even more surplus. Successful capitalists usually make more than enough both to reinvest in expansion and satisfy their lust for pleasure. But the result of perpetual reinvestment is the expansion of surplus production. Even more important, it entails expansion at a compound rate—hence all the logistical growth curves (money, capital, output, and population) that attach to the history of capital accumulation.

The politics of capitalism are affected by the perpetual need to find profitable terrains for capital surplus production and absorption. In this the capitalist faces a number of obstacles to continuous and trouble-free expansion. If there is a scarcity of labor and wages are too high, then either existing labor has to be disciplined (technologically induced unemployment or an assault on organized working class power—such as that set in motion by Thatcher and Reagan in the 1980s—are two prime methods) or fresh labor forces must be found (by immigration, export of capital, or proletarianization of hitherto independent elements in the population). New means of production in general and new natural resources in particular must be found. This puts increasing pressure on the natural environment to yield up the necessary raw materials and absorb the inevitable wastes. The coercive laws of competition also force new technologies and organizational forms to come on line all the time, since capitalists with higher productivity can out-compete those using inferior methods. Innovations define new wants and needs, and reduce the turnover time of capital and the friction of distance. This extends the geographical range over which the capitalist is free to search for expanded labor supplies, raw materials, and so on. If there is not enough purchasing power in an existing market, then new markets must be found by expanding foreign trade, promoting new products and lifestyles, creating new credit instruments and debt-financed state expenditures. If, finally, the profit rate is too low, then state regulation of "ruinous competition," monopolization (mergers and acquisitions), and capital exports to fresh pastures provide ways out.

If any one of the above barriers to continuous capital circulation and expansion becomes impossible to circumvent, then capital accumulation is blocked and capitalists face a crisis. Capital cannot be profitably reinvested, accumulation stagnates or ceases, and capital is devalued (lost) and in some instances even physically destroyed. Devaluation can take a number of forms. Surplus commodities can be devalued or destroyed, productive capacity and assets can be written down in value and left unemployed, or money itself can be devalued through inflation. And in a crisis, of course, labor stands to be devalued through massive unemployment. In what ways, then, has capitalist urbanization been driven by the need to circumvent these barriers and to expand the terrain of profitable capitalist activity? I argue here that it plays a particularly active role (along with other phenomena such as military expenditures) in absorbing the surplus product that capitalists are perpetually producing in their search for surplus value.[4]

Consider, first, the case of Second Empire Paris. The crisis of 1848 was one of the first clear crises of unemployed surplus capital and surplus labor side-by-side, and it was Europe-wide. It struck particularly hard in Paris, and the result was an abortive revolution on the part of unemployed workers and those bourgeois utopians who saw a social republic as the antidote to capitalist greed and inequality. The republican bourgeoisie violently repressed the revolutionaries but failed to resolve the crisis. The result was the ascent to power of Louis Bonaparte, who engineered a coup in 1851 and proclaimed himself emperor in 1852. To survive politically, the authoritarian emperor resorted to widespread political repression of alternative political movements, but he also knew that he had to deal with the capital surplus absorption problem, and this he did by announcing a vast program of infrastructural investment both at home and abroad. Abroad this meant the construction of railroads throughout Europe and down into the Orient, as well as support for grand works such as the Suez Canal. At home it meant consolidating the railway network, building ports and harbors, draining marshes, and the like. But above all it entailed the reconfiguration of the urban infrastructure of Paris. Bonaparte brought Haussmann to Paris to take charge of the public works in 1853.

Haussmann clearly understood that his mission was to help solve the surplus capital and unemployment problem by way of urbanization. The rebuilding of Paris absorbed huge quantities of labor and capital by the standards of the time and, coupled with authoritarian suppression of the aspirations of the Parisian labor force, was a primary vehicle of social stabilization. Haussmann drew upon the utopian plans (by Fourierists and Saint-Simonians) for reshaping Paris that had been debated in the 1840s, but with one big difference: he transformed the scale at which the urban process was imagined. When the architect Hittorf showed Haussmann his plans for a new boulevard, Haussmann threw them back at him, saying "not wide enough ... you have it 40 meters wide and I want it 120." Haussmann thought of the city on a grander scale, annexed the suburbs, and redesigned whole neighborhoods (such as Les Halles) rather than just bits and pieces of the urban fabric. He changed the city wholesale rather than piecemeal. To do this, he needed new financial institutions and debt instruments constructed on Saint-Simonian lines (the Crédit Mobilier and Immobilière). What he did in effect was to help resolve the capital surplus disposal problem by setting up a Keynesian system of debt-financed infrastructural urban improvements.

The system worked very well for some fifteen years, and it entailed not only a transformation of urban infrastructures but the construction of a whole new urban way of life and the construction of a new kind of urban persona. Paris became "the city of light," the great center of consumption, tourism and pleasure—the cafés, the department stores, the fashion industry, the grand expositions all changed the urban way of life in ways that could absorb vast surpluses through crass consumerism (which offended traditionalists and excluded workers alike). But then, in 1868, the overextended and increasingly speculative financial system and credit structures on which this was based crashed. Haussmann was forced from power. In desperation, Napoleon III went to war against Bismarck's Germany, and lost. In the vacuum that followed arose the Paris Commune, one of the greatest revolutionary episodes in capitalist urban history. The Commune was wrought in part out of a nostalgia for the urban world that Haussmann had destroyed (shades of the 1848 Revolution) and the desire to take back their city on the part of those dispossessed by Haussmann's works. But the Commune also articulated conflictual forward-looking visions of alternative socialist (as opposed to monopoly capitalist) modernities that pitted ideals of centralized hierarchical control (the Jacobin current) against decentralized anarchist visions of popular control (led by the Proudhonists). In 1872, in the midst of intense recriminations over who was at fault for the loss of the Commune, there occurred the radical political break between the Marxists and the anarchists that, to this day, still unfortunately divides so much of the left opposition to capitalism.[5]

Fast-forward now to the United States in 1942. The capital surplus disposal problem that had seemed so intractable in the 1930s (and the unemployment that went with it) was temporarily resolved by the huge mobilization for the war effort. But everyone was fearful as to what would happen after the war. Politically the situation was dangerous. The federal government was in effect running a nationalized economy (and was doing so very efficiently), and the United States was in alliance with the communist Soviet Union in the war against fascism. Strong social movements with socialist inclinations had emerged in response to the depression of the 1930s, and sympathizers were integrated into the war effort. We all know the subsequent history of the politics of McCarthyism and the Cold War (abundant signs of which were there in 1942). As under Louis Bonaparte, a hefty dose of political repression was evidently called for by the ruling classes of the time to reassert their power. But what of the capital surplus disposal problem?

In 1942 there appeared a lengthy evaluation of Haussmann's efforts in an architectural journal. It documented in detail what he had done that was so compelling and attempted an analysis of his mistakes. The article was by none other than Robert Moses, who after World War II did to the whole New York metropolitan region what Haussmann had done to Paris.[6] That is, Moses changed the scale of thinking about the urban process and—through the system of (debt-financed) highways and infrastructural transformations, through suburbanization, and through the total re-engineering not just of the city but of the whole metropolitan region—he defined a way to absorb the surplus product and thereby resolve the capital surplus absorption problem. This process, when taken nation-wide, as it was in all the major metropolitan centers of the United States (yet another transformation of scale), played a crucial role in the stabilization of global capitalism after World War II (this was a period when the United States could afford to power the whole global non-communist economy through running trade deficits).

The suburbanization of the United States was not merely a matter of new infrastructures. As in Second Empire Paris, it entailed a radical transformation in lifestyles and produced a whole new way of life in which new products—from suburban tract housing to refrigerators and air conditioners, as well as two cars in the driveway and an enormous increase in the consumption of oil—all played their part in the absorption of the surplus. Suburbanization (alongside militarization) thus played a critical role in helping to absorb the surplus in the post-war years. But it did so at the cost of hollowing out the central cities and leaving them bereft of a sustainable economic basis, thus producing the so-called "urban crisis" of the 1960s, defined by revolts of impacted minorities (chiefly

African-American) in the inner cities, who were denied access to the new prosperity.

Not only were the central cities in revolt. Traditionalists increasingly rallied around Jane Jacobs and sought to counter the brutal modernism of Moses's large-scale projects with a different kind of urban aesthetic that focused on local neighborhood development, and on the historical preservation, and ultimately gentrification, of older areas. But by then the suburbs had been built, and the radical transformation in lifestyle that this betokened had all manner of social consequences, leading feminists, for example, to proclaim the suburb and its lifestyle as the locus of all their primary discontents. As had happened to Haussmann, a crisis began to unfold such that Moses fell from grace, and his solutions came to be seen as inappropriate and unacceptable towards the end of the 1960s. And if the Haussmannization of Paris had a role in explaining the dynamics of the Paris Commune, so the soulless qualities of suburban living played a critical role in the dramatic movements of 1968 in the United States, as discontented white middle-class students went into a phase of revolt, seeking alliances with other marginalized groups and rallying against US imperialism to create a movement to build another kind of world, including a different kind of urban experience (though, again, anarchistic and libertarian currents were pitted against demands for hierarchical and centralized alternatives).[7]

Along with the '68 revolt came a financial crisis. It was partly global (with the collapse of the Bretton Woods agreements), but it also originated within the credit institutions that had powered the property boom in the preceding decades. This crisis gathered momentum at the end of the 1960s, until the whole capitalist system crashed into a major global crisis, led by the bursting of the global property market bubble in 1973, followed by the fiscal bankruptcy of New York City in 1975. The dark days of the 1970s had arrived, and the question then was how to rescue capitalism from its own contradictions. In this, if history was to be any guide, the urban process was bound to play a significant role. As William Tabb showed, the working through of the New York fiscal crisis of 1975, orchestrated by an uneasy alliance between state powers and financial institutions, pioneered a neoliberal answer to this question: the class power of capital was to be protected at the expense of working-class standards of living, while the market was deregulated to do its work. But the question then was how to revive the capacity to absorb the surpluses that capitalism must produce if it was to survive.[8]

Fast-forward once again to our current conjuncture. International capitalism was on a roller-coaster of regional crises and crashes (East and Southeast Asia in 1997–98, Russia in 1998, Argentina in 2001, and so on) until it experienced a global crash in 2008. What has been the role of urbanization in this history? In the United States it was accepted wisdom until 2008 that the housing market was an important stabilizer of the economy, particularly after the high-tech crash of the late 1990s. The property market absorbed a great deal of the surplus capital directly through new construction (of both inner-city and suburban housing and new office spaces), while the rapid inflation of housing asset prices, backed by a profligate wave of mortgage refinancing at historically low rates of interest, boosted the internal US market for consumer goods and services. The global market was stabilized partly through US urban expansion and speculation in property markets, as the US ran huge trade deficits with the rest of the world, borrowing around $2 billion a day to fuel its insatiable consumerism and the debt-financed wars in Afghanistan and Iraq during the first decade of the twenty-first century.

But the urban process underwent another transformation of scale. In short, it went global. So we cannot focus merely on the US. Property market booms in Britain, Ireland, and Spain, as well as in many other countries, helped power the capitalist dynamic in ways that broadly paralleled that in the US. The urbanization of China over the last twenty years, as we shall see in Chapter 2, has been of a radically different character, with a heavy focus on building infrastructures. Its pace picked up enormously after a brief recession in 1997 or so. More than a hundred cities have passed the 1 million population mark in the last twenty years, and small villages, like Shenzhen, have become huge metropolises of 6 to 10 million people. Industrialization was at first concentrated in the special economic zones, but then rapidly diffused outwards to any municipality willing to absorb the surplus capital from abroad and plough back the earnings into rapid expansion. Vast infrastructural projects, such as dams and highways—again, all debt-financed—are transforming the landscape.[9] Equally vast shopping malls, science parks, airports, container ports, pleasure palaces of all kinds, and all manner of newly minted cultural institutions, along with gated communities and golf courses, dot the Chinese landscape in the midst of overcrowded urban dormitories for the massive labor reserves being mobilized from the impoverished rural regions that supply the migrant labor. As we shall see, the consequences of this urbanization process for the global economy and for the absorption of surplus capital have been huge.

But China is only one epicenter for an urbanization process that has now become genuinely global, in part through the astonishing global integration of financial markets that use their flexibility to debt-finance urban projects from Dubai to São Paulo and from Madrid and Mumbai to Hong Kong and London. The Chinese central bank, for example, has been active in the secondary mortgage market in the US, while Goldman Sachs has been involved in the surging property markets in Mumbai and Hong Kong capital has invested in Baltimore. Almost every city in the world has witnessed a building boom for the rich—often of a distressingly similar character—in the midst of a flood of impoverished migrants converging on cities as a rural peasantry is dispossessed through the industrialization and commercialization of agriculture.

These building booms have been evident in Mexico City, Santiago in Chile, in Mumbai, Johannesburg, Seoul, Taipei, Moscow, and all over Europe (Spain's being most dramatic), as well as in the cities of the core capitalist countries such as London, Los Angeles, San Diego, and New York (where more large-scale urban projects were in motion in 2007 under the billionaire Bloomberg's administration than ever before). Astonishing, spectacular, and in some respects criminally absurd urbanization projects have emerged in the Middle East in places like Dubai and Abu Dhabi as a way of mopping up the capital surpluses arising from oil wealth in the most conspicuous, socially unjust and environmentally wasteful ways possible (such as an indoor ski slope in a hot desert environment). We are here looking at yet another transformation in scale of the urban process—one that makes it hard to grasp that what may be going on globally is in principle similar to the processes that Haussmann managed so expertly for a while in Second Empire Paris.

But this urbanization boom has depended, as did all the others before it, on the construction of new financial institutions and arrangements to organize the credit required to sustain it. Financial innovations set in train in the 1980s, particularly the securitization and packaging of local mortgages for sale to investors world-wide, and the setting up of new financial institutions to facilitate a secondary mortgage market and to hold collateralized debt obligations, has played a crucial role. The benefits of this were legion: it spread risk and permitted surplus savings pools easier access to surplus housing demand, and also, by virtue of its coordinations, it brought aggregate interest rates down (while generating immense fortunes for the financial intermediaries who worked these wonders). But spreading risk does not eliminate risk. Furthermore, the fact that risk can be spread so widely encourages even riskier local behaviors, because the risk can be transferred elsewhere. Without adequate risk-assessment controls, the mortgage market got out of hand, and what happened to the Péreire Brothers in 1867–68 and to the fiscal profligacy of New York City in the early 1970s was then repeated in the sub-prime mortgage and housing asset-value crisis of 2008. The crisis was concentrated in the first instance in and around US cities (though similar signs could be seen in Britain), with particularly serious implications for low-income African-Americans and single head-of-household women in the inner cities. It also affected those who, unable to afford the skyrocketing housing prices in the urban centers, particularly in the US southwest, moved to the semi-periphery of metropolitan areas to take up speculatively built tract housing at initially easy credit rates, but who then faced escalating commuting costs with rising oil prices and soaring mortgage payments as market-interest rates kicked in. This crisis, with vicious local impacts on urban life and infrastructures (whole neighborhoods in cities like Cleveland, Baltimore, and Detroit have been devastated by the foreclosure wave), threatened the whole architecture of the global financial system, and triggered a major recession to boot. The parallels with the 1970s are, to put it mildly, uncanny (including the immediate easy-money response of the US Federal Reserve, which is almost certain to generate strong inflationary threats, as happened in the late 1970s, sometime in the future).

But the situation is far more complicated now and it is an open question whether a serious crash in the United States can be compensated for elsewhere (for example, by China). Uneven geographical development may once again rescue the system from a totalizing global crash, as it did in the 1990s, though it is the United States that is this time at the center of the problem. But the financial system is also much more tightly coupled temporally than it ever was before.[10] Computer-driven split-second trading, once it does go off-track, always threatens to create some great divergence in the market (it has produced incredible volatility in stock markets) that will produce a massive crisis requiring a total rethink of how finance capital and money markets work, including in relation to urbanization.

As in all the preceding phases, this most recent radical expansion of the urban process has brought with it incredible transformations in lifestyles. Quality of urban life has become a commodity for those with money, as has the city itself in a world where consumerism, tourism, cultural and knowledge-based industries, as well as perpetual resort to the economy of the spectacle, have become major aspects of urban political economy, even in India and China. The postmodernist penchant for encouraging the formation of market niches, both in urban lifestyle choices and in consumer habits, and cultural forms, surrounds the contemporary urban experience with an aura of freedom of choice in the market, provided you have the money and can protect yourself from the privatization of wealth redistribution through burgeoning criminal activity and preda-tory fraudulent practices (which have everywhere escalated). Shopping malls, multiplexes, and box stores proliferate (the production of each has become big business), as do fast-food and artisanal market places, boutique cultures and, as Sharon Zukin slyly notes, "pacification by cap-puccino." Even the incoherent, bland, and monotonous suburban tract development that continues to dominate in many areas, now gets its anti-dote in a "new urbanism" movement that touts the sale of community and a boutique lifestyle as a developer product to fulfill urban dreams. This is a world in which the neoliberal ethic of intense possessive indi-vidualism can become the template for human personality socialization. The impact is increasing individualistic isolation, anxiety, and neurosis in the midst of one of the greatest social achievements (at least judging by its enormous scale and all-embracing character) ever constructed in human history for the realization of our hearts' desire.

But the fissures within the system are also all too evident. We increasingly live in divided, fragmented, and conflict-prone cities. How we view the world and define possibilities depends on which side of the tracks we are on and on what kinds of consumerism we have access to. In the past decades, the neoliberal turn has restored class power to rich elites.[11] In a single year several hedge fund managers in New York raked in $3 billion in personal remuneration, and Wall Street bonuses have soared for individuals over the last few years from around $5 million towards the $50 million mark for top players (putting real estate prices in Manhattan out of sight). Fourteen billionaires have emerged in Mexico since the neoliberal turn in the late 1980s, and Mexico now boasts the richest man on earth, Carlos Slim, at the same time as the incomes of the poor in that country have either stagnated or diminished. As of the end of 2009 (after the worst of the crash was over), there were 115 billionaires in China, 101 in Russia, 55 in India, 52 in Germany, 32 in Britain, and 30 in Brazil, in addition to the 413 in the United States.[12] The results of this increasing polarization in the distribution of wealth and power are indelibly etched into the spatial forms of our cities, which increasingly become cities of fortified fragments, of gated communities and privatized public spaces kept under constant surveillance. The neoliberal protection of private property rights and their values becomes a hegemonic form of politics, even for the lower middle class. In the developing world in particular, the city

> is splitting into different separated parts, with the apparent formation of many "microstates." Wealthy neighborhoods provided with all kinds of services, such as exclusive schools, golf courses, tennis courts and private police patrolling the area around the clock intertwine with illegal settlements where water is available only at public fountains, no sanitation system exists, electricity is pirated by a privileged few, the roads become mud streams whenever it rains, and where house-sharing is the norm. Each fragment appears to live and function autonomously, sticking firmly to what it has been able to grab in the daily fight for survival.[13]

Under these conditions, ideals of urban identity, citizenship, and belonging, of a coherent urban politics, already threatened by the spreading malaise of the individualistic neoliberal ethic, become much harder to sustain. Even the idea that the city might function as a collective body politic, a site within and from which progressive social movements might emanate, appears, at least on the surface, increasingly implausible. Yet there are in fact all manner of urban social movements in evidence seeking to overcome the isolations and to reshape the city in a different social image from that given by the powers of developers backed by finance, corporate capital, and an increasingly entrepreneurially minded local state apparatus. Even relatively conservative urban administrations are seeking ways to use their powers to experiment with new ways of both producing the urban and of democratizing governance. Is there an urban alternative and, if so, from where might it come?

Surplus absorption through urban transformation has, however, an even darker aspect. It has entailed repeated bouts of urban restructuring through "creative destruction." This nearly always has a class dimension, since it is usually the poor, the underprivileged, and those marginalized from political power that suffer first and foremost from this process. Violence is required to achieve the new urban world on the wreckage of the old. Haussmann tore through the old Parisian impoverished quarters, using powers of expropriation for supposedly public benefit, and did so in the name of civic improvement, environmental restoration, and urban renovation. He deliberately engineered the removal of much of the working class and other unruly elements, along with insalubrious industries, from Paris's city center, where they constituted a threat to public order, public health and, of course, political power. He created an urban form where it was believed (incorrectly, as it turned out, in 1871) sufficient levels of surveillance and military control were possible so as to ensure that revolutionary movements could easily be controlled by military power. But, as Engels pointed out in 1872,

> In reality, the bourgeoisie has only one method of solving the housing question after its fashion—that is to say, of solving it in such a way that the solution perpetually renews the question anew. This method is called "Haussmann" [by which] I mean the practice that has now become general of making breaches in the working class quarters of our big towns, and particularly in areas which are centrally situated, quite apart from whether this is done from considerations of public health or for beautifying the town, or owing to the demand for big centrally situated business premises, or, owing to traffic requirements, such as the laying

down of railways, streets (which sometimes seem to have the aim of making barricade fighting more difficult) ... No matter how different the reasons may be, the result is always the same; the scandalous alleys disappear to the accompaniment of lavish self-praise by the bourgeoisie on account of this tremendous success, but they appear again immediately somewhere else ... The breeding places of disease, the infamous holes and cellars in which the capitalist mode of production confines our workers night after night, are not abolished; they are merely *shifted elsewhere!* The same economic necessity that produced them in the first place, produces them in the next place.[14]

Actually it took more than a hundred years to complete the bourgeois conquest of central Paris, with the consequences that we have seen in recent years of uprisings and mayhem in those isolated suburbs within which the marginalized immigrants and the unemployed workers and youth are increasingly trapped. The sad point here, of course, is that the processes Engels described recur again and again in capitalist urban history. Robert Moses "took a meat axe to the Bronx" (in his infamous words), and long and loud were the lamentations of neighborhood groups and movements, which eventually coalesced around the rhetoric of Jane Jacobs, at the unimaginable destruction not only of valued urban fabric but also of whole communities of residents and their long-established networks of social integration.[15] But in the New York and Parisian case, once the brutal power of state expropriations had been successfully resisted and contained by the agitations of '68, a far more insidious and cancerous process of transformation occurred through fiscal disciplining of democratic urban governments, land markets, property speculation, and the sorting of land to those uses that generated the highest possible financial rate of return under the land's "highest and best use." Engels understood all too well what this process was about too:

The growth of the big modern cities gives the land in certain areas, particularly in those areas which are centrally situated, an artificially and colossally increasing value; the buildings erected on these areas depress this value instead of increasing it, because they no longer belong to the changed circumstances. They are pulled down and replaced by others. This takes place above all with workers' houses which are situated centrally and whose rents, even with the greatest overcrowding, can never, or only very slowly, increase above a certain maximum. They are pulled down and in their stead shops, warehouses and public building are erected.[16]

It is depressing to think that all of this was written in 1872, for Engels's description applies directly to contemporary urban processes in much of Asia (Delhi, Seoul, Mumbai) as well as to the contemporary gentrification of, say, Harlem and Brooklyn in New York. A process of displacement and dispossession, in short, also lies at the core of the urban process under capitalism. This is the mirror image of capital absorption through urban redevelopment. Consider the case of Mumbai, where there are 6 million people considered officially as slum-dwellers settled on land for the most part without legal title (the places where they live are left blank on all maps of the city). With the attempt to turn Mumbai into a global financial center to rival Shanghai, the property development boom gathers pace and the land the slum-dwellers occupy appears increasingly valuable. The value of the land in Dharavi, one of the most prominent slums in Mumbai, is put at $2 billion, and the pressure to clear the slum (for environmental and social reasons that mask the land grab) is mounting daily. Financial powers, backed by the state, push for forcible slum clearance, in some cases violently taking possession of a terrain occupied for a whole generation by the slum-dwellers. Capital accumulation on the land through real estate activity booms as land is acquired at almost no cost. Do the people forced out get compensation? The lucky ones get a bit. But while the Indian constitution specifies that the state has the obligation to protect the lives and well-being of the whole population irrespective of caste and class, and to guarantee rights to livelihood housing and shelter, the Indian Supreme Court has issued both non-judgments and judgments that rewrite this constitutional requirement. Since the slum-dwellers are illegal occupants and many cannot definitively prove their long-term residence on the land, they have no right to compensation. To concede that right, says the Supreme Court, would be tantamount to rewarding pickpockets for their actions. So the slum-dwellers either resist and fight or move with their few belongings to camp out on the highway margins, or wherever they can find a tiny space.[17] Similar examples of dispossession (though less brutal and more legalistic) can be found in the

US, through the abuse of rights of eminent domain to displace long-term residents in reasonable housing in favor of higher-order land uses (such as condominiums and box stores). Challenged in the US Supreme Court, the liberal justices carried the day against the conservatives in saying it was perfectly constitutional for local jurisdictions to behave in this way in order to increase their property tax base.

In Seoul in the 1990s, the construction companies and developers hired goon squads of sumo-wrestler types to invade whole neighborhoods and smash down with sledgehammers not only the housing but also all the possessions of those who had built their own housing on the hillsides of the city in the 1950s, on what by the 1990s had become high-value land. Most of those hillsides are now covered with high-rise towers that show no trace of the brutal processes of land clearance that permitted their construction. In China millions are being dispossessed of the spaces they have long occupied. Lacking private property rights, they can be simply removed from the land by the state by fiat, offered a minor cash payment to help them on their way (before the land is turned over to developers at a high rate of profit). In some instances people move willingly, but widespread resistance is also reported, the usual response to which is brutal repression by the Communist Party. In the Chinese case, it is often populations on the rural margins who are displaced, illustrating the significance of Lefebvre's argument, presciently laid out in the 1960s, that the clear distinction that once existed between the urban and the rural was gradually fading into a set of porous spaces of uneven geographical development under the hegemonic command of capital and the state. In China, rural communes on urban fringes went from the backbreaking and impoverishing labor of growing cabbages to the leisurely status of urban rentiers (or at least their commune party leaders did) growing condominiums, as it were, overnight. This is the case also in India, where the special economic development zones policy now favored by central and state governments is leading to violence against agricultural producers, the grossest of which was the massacre at Nandigram in West Bengal, orchestrated by the ruling Marxist political party, to make way for large-scale Indonesian capital that is as much interested in urban property development as it is in industrial development. Private property rights in this case provided no protection.

And so it is with the seemingly progressive proposal of awarding private property rights to squatter populations in order to offer them the assets that will permit them to emerge out of poverty. This is the sort of proposal now mooted for Rio's favelas, but the problem is that the poor, beset with insecurity of income and frequent financial difficulties, can easily be persuaded to trade in that asset for a cash payment at a relatively low price (the rich typically refuse to give up their valued assets at any price, which is why Moses could take a meat axe to the low-income Bronx but not to affluent Park Avenue). My bet is that, if present trends continue, within fifteen years all those hillsides now occupied by favelas will be covered by high-rise condominiums with fabulous views over Rio's bay, while the erstwhile favela-dwellers will have been filtered off to live in some remote periphery.[18] The long-term effect of Margaret Thatcher's privatization of social housing in central London has been to create a rent and housing price structure throughout the metropolitan area that precludes lower-income and now even middle-class people from having access to housing anywhere near the urban center. The affordable housing problem, like the poverty and accessibility problem, has indeed been moved around.

These examples warn us of the existence of a whole battery of seemingly "progressive" solutions that not only move the problem around but actually strengthen while simultaneously lengthening the golden chain that imprisons vulnerable and marginalized populations within orbits of capital circulation and accumulation. Hernando de Soto argues influentially that it is the lack of clear property rights that holds the poor down in misery in so much of the global south (ignoring the fact that poverty is abundantly in evidence in societies where clear property rights are readily established). To be sure, there will be instances where the granting of such rights in Rio's favelas or in Lima's slums liberates individual energies and entrepreneurial endeavors leading to personal advancement. But the concomitant effect is often to destroy collective and non-profit-maximizing modes of social solidarity and mutual support, while any aggregate effect will almost certainly be nullified in the absence of secure and adequately remunerative employment. In Cairo, Elyachar, for example, notes how these seemingly progressive policies create a "market of dispossession" that in effect seeks to suck value out of a moral economy based on mutual respect and reciprocity, to the advantage of capitalist institutions.[19]

Much the same commentary applies to the micro-credit and micro-finance solutions to global poverty now touted so persuasively among the Washington financial institutions. Micro-credit in its social incarnation (as originally envisaged by the Nobel Peace Prize winner, Yunus) has indeed opened up new possibilities and had a significant impact on gender relations, with positive consequences for women in countries such as India and Bangladesh. But it does so by imposing systems of collective responsibility for debt repayments that can imprison rather than liberate. In the world of micro-finance as articulated by the Washington institutions (as opposed to the social and more philanthropic orientation of micro-credit proposed by Yunus), the effect is to generate high-yielding sources of income (with interest rates of at least 18 percent, and often far higher) for global financial institutions, in the midst of an emergent marketing structure that permits multinational corporations access to the massive aggregate market constituted by the 2 billion people living on less that $2 a day. This huge "market at the bottom of the pyramid," as it is called in business circles, is to be penetrated on behalf of big business by constructing elaborate networks of salespeople (chiefly women) linked through a marketing chain from multinational warehouse to street vendors.[20] The salespeople form a collective of social relations, all responsible for each other, set up for guaranteeing repayment of the debt plus interest that allows them to buy the commodities that they subsequently market piecemeal. As with granting private property rights, almost certainly some people (and in this case mostly women) may even go on to become relatively well-off, while notorious problems of difficulty of access of the poor to consumer products at reasonable prices will be attenuated. But this is no solution to the urban-impacted poverty problem. Most participants in the micro-finance system will be reduced to the status of debt peonage, locked into a badly remunerated bridge position between the multinational corporations and the impoverished populations of the urban slums, with the advantage always going to the multinational corporation. This is the kind of structure that will block the exploration of more productive alternatives. It certainly does not proffer any right to the city.

Urbanization, we may conclude, has played a crucial role in the absorption of capital surpluses and has done so at ever-increasing geographical scales, but at the price of burgeoning processes of creative destruction that entail the dispossession of the urban masses of any right to the city whatsoever. Periodically this ends in revolt, as in Paris in 1871, when the dispossessed rose up seeking to reclaim the city they had lost. The urban social movements of 1968, from Paris and Bangkok to Mexico City and Chicago, likewise sought to define a different way of urban living from that which was being imposed upon them by capitalist developers and the state. If, as seems likely, the fiscal difficulties in the current conjuncture mount and the hitherto successful neoliberal, postmodernist, and consumerist phase of capitalist absorption of the surplus through urbanization is at an end, and if a broader crisis ensues, then the question arises: Where is our '68 or, even more dramatically, our version of the Commune?

By analogy with transformations in the fiscal system, the political answer is bound to be much more complex in our times precisely because the urban process is now global in scope and wracked with all manner of fissures, insecurities, and uneven geographical developments. But cracks in the system are, as Leonard Cohen once sang, "what lets the light in." Signs of revolt are everywhere (the unrest in China and India is chronic, civil wars rage in Africa, Latin America is in ferment, autonomy movements are emerging all over the place, and even in the US the political signs suggest that most of the population is saying "enough is enough" with respect to rabid inequalities). Any of these revolts could suddenly become contagious. Unlike the fiscal system, however, the urban and peri-urban social movements of opposition, of which there are many around the world, are not tightly coupled at all. Indeed, many have no connection to each other. It is unlikely, therefore, that a single spark will, as the Weather Underground once dreamed, spark a prairie fire. It will take something far more systematic than that. But if these various oppositional movements did somehow come together—coalesce, for example, around the slogan of the right to the city—then what should they demand?

The answer to the last question is simple enough: greater democratic control over the production and use of the surplus. Since the urban process is a major channel of use, then the right to the city is constituted by establishing democratic control over the deployment of the surpluses through urbanization. To have a surplus product is not a bad thing: indeed, in many situations a surplus is crucial to adequate survival. Throughout capitalist history, some of the surplus value created has been taxed away by the state, and in social-democratic phases that proportion rose significantly, putting much of the surplus under state control. The whole neoliberal project over the last thirty years has been oriented towards privatization of control over the surplus. The data for all OECD countries show, however, that the share of gross output taken by the state has been roughly constant since the 1970s. The main achievement of the neoliberal assault, then, has been to prevent the state share expanding in the way it did in the 1960s. One further response has been to create new systems of governance that integrate state and corporate interests and, through the application of money power, assure that control over the disbursement of the surplus through the state apparatus favors corporate capital and the upper classes in the shaping of the urban process. Increasing the share of the surplus under state control will only work if the state itself is both reformed and brought back under popular democratic control.

Increasingly, we see the right to the city falling into the hands of private or quasi-private interests. In New York City, for example, we have a billionaire mayor, Michael Bloomberg, who is reshaping the city along lines favorable to the developers, to Wall Street and transnational capitalist class elements, while continuing to sell the city as an optimal location for high-value businesses and a fantastic destination for tourists, thus turning Manhattan in effect into one vast gated community for the rich. (His developmental slogan, ironically, has been "Building Like Moses with Jane Jacobs in Mind."[21]) In Seattle a billionaire like Paul Allen calls the shots, and in Mexico City the wealthiest man in the world, Carlos Slim, has the downtown streets re-cobbled to suit the tourist gaze. And it is not only affluent individuals who exercise direct power. In the town of New Haven, strapped for any resources for urban reinvestment of its own, it is Yale University, one of the wealthiest universities in the world, that is redesigning much of the urban fabric to suit its needs. Johns Hopkins is doing the same for East Baltimore, and Columbia University plans to do so for areas of New York (sparking neighborhood resistance movements in both cases, as has the attempted land-grab in Dharavi). The actually existing right to the city, as it is now constituted, is far too narrowly confined, in most cases in the hands of a small political and economic elite who are in a position to shape the city more and more after their own particular needs and hearts' desire.

But let us look at this situation more structurally. In January every year an estimate is published of the total of Wall Street bonuses earned for all the hard work the financiers engaged in during the previous year. In 2007, a disastrous year for financial markets by any measure (though by no means as bad as the year that followed), the bonuses added up to $33.2 billion, only 2 percent less than the year before (not a bad rate of remuneration for messing up the world's financial system). In mid-summer of 2007, the Federal Reserve and the European Central Bank pumped billions of short-term credit into the financial system to ensure its stability, and the Federal Reserve dramatically lowered interest rates as the year progressed every time the Wall Street markets threatened to fall precipitously. Meanwhile, some 2 or perhaps 3 million people—mainly a mix of single-woman-headed households, African-Americans in central cities, and marginalized white populations in the urban semi-periphery—have been or are about to be rendered homeless by foreclosures. Many city neighborhoods and even whole peri-urban communities in the United States were boarded up and vandalized, wrecked by the predatory lending practices of the financial institutions. This population received no bonuses. Indeed, since foreclosure means forgiveness of debt, and that is regarded as income, many of those foreclosed on face a hefty income tax bill for money they never had in their possession. This awful asymmetry poses the following question: Why did the Federal Reserve and the US Treasury not extend medium-term liquidity help to the households threatened with foreclosure until mortgage restructuring at reasonable rates could resolve much of the problem? The ferocity of the credit crisis would have been mitigated, and impoverished people and the neighborhoods they inhabited would have been protected. Furthermore, the global financial system would not have teetered on the brink of total insolvency, as happened a year later. To be sure, this would have extended the mission of the Federal Reserve beyond its normal remit, and gone against the neoliberal ideological rule that, in the event of a conflict between the well-being of financial institutions and that of the people, then the people should be left to one side. It would also have gone against capitalist class preferences with respect to income distribution and neoliberal notions of personal responsibility. But just look at the price that was paid for observing such rules and the senseless creative destruction that resulted from it. Surely something can and should be done to reverse these political choices?

But we have yet to see a coherent oppositional movement to all of this in the twenty-first century. There is, of course, a multitude of diverse urban struggles and urban social movements (in the broadest sense of that term, including movements in the rural hinterlands) already in existence. Urban innovations with respect to environmental sustainability, cultural incorporation of immigrants, and urban design of public housing spaces are observable around the world in abundance. But they have yet to converge on the singular aim of gaining greater control over the uses of the surplus (let alone over the conditions of its production). One step, though by no means final, towards unification of these struggles is to focus sharply on those moments of creative destruction where the economy of wealth-accumulation piggy-backs violently on the economy of dispossession, and there proclaim on behalf of the dispossessed their right to the city—their right to change the world, to change life, and to reinvent the city more after their hearts' desire. That collective right, as both a working slogan and a political ideal, brings us back to the age-old question of who it is that commands the inner connection between urbanization and surplus production and use. Perhaps, after all, Lefebvre was right, more than forty years ago, to insist that the revolution in our times has to be urban—or nothing.

CHAPTER TWO

The Urban Roots of Capitalist Crises

In an article in the *New York Times* on February 5, 2011, entitled "Housing Bubbles Are Few and Far Between," Robert Shiller, the economist who many consider the great housing expert in the US, given his role in the construction of the Case-Shiller index of housing prices, reassured everyone that the recent housing bubble was a "rare event, not to be repeated for many decades." The "enormous housing bubble" of the early 2000s "isn't comparable to any national or international housing cycle in history. Previous bubbles have been smaller and more regional." The only reasonable parallels, he asserted, were the land bubbles that occurred in the US back in the late 1830s and in the 1850s.[1]

This is, as I shall show, an astonishingly inaccurate and dangerous reading of capitalist history. The fact that it passed so unremarked testifies to a serious blind spot in contemporary economic thinking. Unfortunately, it also turns out to be an equally blind spot in Marxist political economy. The housing crash of 2007–10 in the US was certainly deeper and longer than most—indeed, it may well mark the end of an era in US economic history—but it was by no means unprecedented in its relation to macroeconomic disturbances in the world market, and there are several signs that it is about to be repeated.

Conventional economics routinely treats investment in the built environment in general, and in housing in particular, along with urbanization, as some side-bar to the more important affairs that go on in some fictional entity called "the national economy." The sub-field of "urban economics" is thus the arena where inferior economists go while the big guns ply their macroeconomic trading skills elsewhere. Even when the latter notice urban processes, they make it seem as if spatial reorganizations, regional development, and the building of cities are merely some on-the-ground outcome of larger-scale processes that remain unaffected by that which they produce.[2] Thus, in the 2009 World Bank Development Report, which, for the first time ever, took economic geography and urban development seriously, the authors did so without a hint that anything could possibly go so catastrophically wrong as to spark a crisis in the economy as a whole. Written by economists (without consulting geographers, historians, or urban sociologists), its aim was supposedly to explore the "influence of geography on economic opportunity" and to elevate "space and place from mere undercurrents in policy to a major focus."

The authors were actually out to show how the application of the usual nostrums of neoliberal economics to urban affairs (like getting the state out of the business of any serious regulation of land and property markets and minimizing the interventions of urban, regional and spatial planning in the name of social justice and regional equality) was the best way to augment economic growth (in other words, capital accumulation). Though they did have the decency to "regret" that they did not have the time or space to explore in detail the social and environmental consequences of their proposals, they did plainly believe that cities that provide

> fluid land and property markets and other supportive institutions—
> such as protecting property rights, enforcing contracts, and financing
> housing—will more likely flourish over time as the needs of the market
> change. Successful cities have relaxed zoning laws to allow higher-value
> users to bid for the valuable land—and have adopted land use regulations
> to adapt to their changing roles over time.[3]

But land is not a commodity in the ordinary sense. It is a fictitious form of capital that derives from expectations of future rents. Maximizing its yield has driven low- or even moderate-income households out of Manhattan and central London over the last few years, with catastrophic effects on class disparities and the well-being of underprivileged populations. This is what is putting such intense pressure on the high-value land of Dharavi in Mumbai (a so-called slum that the report correctly depicts as a productive human ecosystem). In short, the report advocates the kind of free-market fundamentalism that has spawned a macroeconomic earthquake of the sort we have just passed through (together with its continuing aftershocks) alongside urban social movements of opposition to gentrification, neighborhood destruction, and the use of eminent domain (or more brutal methods) to evict residents to make way for higher-value land uses.

Since the mid 1980s, neoliberal urban policy (applied, for example, across the European Union) concluded that redistributing wealth to less advantaged neighborhoods, cities, and regions was futile, and that resources should instead be channeled to dynamic "entrepreneurial" growth poles. A spatial version of "trickle-down" would then, in the proverbial long run (which never comes), take care of all those pesky regional, spatial, and urban inequalities. Turning the city over to the developers and speculative financiers redounds to the benefit of all! If only the Chinese had liberated land uses in their cities to free market forces, the World Bank Report argued, their economy would have grown even faster than it had!

The World Bank plainly favors speculative capital over people. The idea that a city can do well (in terms of capital accumulation) while its people (apart from a privileged class) and the environment do badly, is never examined. Even worse, the report is deeply complicit with the policies that lay at the root of the crisis of 2007–09. This is particularly odd, given that the report was published six months after the Lehman bankruptcy and nearly two years after the US housing market turned sour and the foreclosure tsunami was clearly identifiable. We are told, for example, without a hint of critical commentary, that

> since the deregulation of financial systems in the second half of the 1980s, market-based housing financing has expanded rapidly. Residential mortgage markets are now equivalent to more than 40 percent of gross domestic product (GDP) in developed countries, but those in developing

countries are much smaller, averaging less than 10 percent of GDP. The public role should be to stimulate well-regulated private involvement … Establishing the legal foundations for simple, enforceable, and prudent mortgage contracts is a good start. When a country's system is more developed and mature, the public sector can encourage a secondary mortgage market, develop financial innovations, and expand the securitization of mortgages. Occupant-owned housing, usually a household's largest single asset by far, is important in wealth creation, social security and politics. People who own their house or who have secure tenure have a larger stake in their community and thus are more likely to lobby for less crime, stronger governance, and better local environmental conditions.[4]

These statements are nothing short of astonishing given recent events. Roll on the sub-prime mortgage business, fueled by pablum myths about the benefits of homeownership for all and the filing away of toxic mortgages in highly rated CDOs to be sold to unsuspecting investors. Roll on endless suburbanization that is both land- and energy-consuming way beyond what is reasonable for the sustained use of planet earth for human habitation! The authors might plausibly maintain that they had no remit to connect their thinking about urbanization with issues of global warming. Along with Alan Greenspan, they could also argue that they were blind-sided by the events of 2007–09, and that they could not be expected to have anticipated anything troubling about the rosy scenario they painted. By inserting the words "prudent" and "well-regulated" into the argument they had, as it were, "hedged" against potential criticism.

But since they cite innumerable "prudentially chosen" historical examples to bolster their neoliberal nostrums, how come they missed that the crisis of 1973 originated in a global property market crash that brought down several banks? Did they not notice that the commercial property-led Savings and Loan crisis of the late 1980s in the United States saw several hundred financial institutions go belly-up at the cost of some US$200 billion to US taxpayers (a situation that so exercised William Isaacs, then chairman of the Federal Deposit Insurance Corporation, that in 1987 he threatened the American Bankers Association with nationalization unless they mended their ways)? That the end of the Japanese boom in 1990 corresponded to a collapse of land prices (still ongoing)? That the Swedish banking system had to be nationalized in 1992 because of excesses in property markets? That one of the triggers for the collapse in East and Southeast Asia in 1997–98 was excessive urban development in Thailand?[5]

Where were the World Bank economists when all this was going on? There have been hundreds of financial crises since 1973 (compared to very few prior to that), and quite a few of them have been property- or urban development–led. And it was pretty clear to almost anyone who thought about it—including, it turns out, Robert Shiller—that something was going badly wrong in US housing markets after 2001 or so. But he saw it as exceptional rather than systemic.[6]

Shiller could well claim, of course, that all of the above other examples were merely regional events. But then so, from the standpoint of the people of Brazil or China, was the housing crisis of 2007–09. The epicenter was the US southwest and Florida (with some spillover in Georgia), along with a few other hot-spots (the grumbling foreclosure crises that began in the late 1990s in poor areas in older cities like Baltimore and Cleveland were too local and "unimportant" because those affected were African-Americans and minorities). Internationally, Spain and Ireland were badly caught out, as was Britain, though to a lesser extent. But there were no serious problems in the property markets in France, Germany, the Netherlands, or Poland, or at that time throughout Asia.

A regional crisis centered in the United States went global, to be sure, in ways that did not happen in the cases of, say, Japan or Sweden in the early 1990s. But the S&L crisis centered on 1987 (the year of a serious stock crash that is typically and erroneously viewed as a totally separate incident) had global ramifications. The same was true of the much-neglected global property market crash of early 1973. Conventional wisdom has it that only the oil price hike in the fall of 1973 mattered. But it turned out that the property crash preceded the oil price hike by six months or more, and the recession was well under way by the fall (see Figure 1). The property market crash spilled over (for obvious revenue reasons) into the fiscal crisis of local states (which would not have happened had the recession been only about oil prices). The subsequent New York City fiscal crisis of 1975 was hugely important because at that time it controlled one of the largest public budgets in the world (prompting pleas from the French president and the West German chancellor to bail

New York City out to avoid a global implosion in financial markets). New York then became the center for the invention of neoliberal practices of gifting moral hazard to the investment banks and making the people pay up through the restructuring of municipal contracts and services. The impact of the most recent property market crash has also carried over into the virtual bankruptcy of states like California, visiting huge stresses in state and municipal government finance and government employment on almost everywhere in the US. The story of the New York City fiscal crisis of the 1970s eerily resembles that of the state of California, which today has the eighth-largest public budget in the world.[7]

The National Bureau of Economic Research has recently unearthed yet another example of the role of property booms in sparking deep crises of capitalism. From a study of real estate data in the 1920s, Goetzmann and Newman "conclude that publically issued real estate securities affected real estate construction activity in the 1920s and the breakdown in their valuation, through the mechanism of the collateral cycle, may have led to the subsequent stock market crash of 1929–30." With respect to housing, Florida, then as now, was an intense center of speculative development, with the nominal value of a building permit increasing by 8,000 percent between 1919 and 1925. Nationally, the estimates of increases in housing values were around 400 percent over roughly the same period. But this was a sideshow compared to commercial development which was almost entirely centered on New York and Chicago, where all manner of financial supports and securitization procedures were concocted to fuel a boom "matched only in the mid-2000s." Even more telling is the graph Goetzmann and Newman compile on tall-building construction in New York City (see Figure 2). The property booms that preceded the crashes of 1929, 1973, 1987, and 2000 stand out like a pikestaff. The buildings we see around us in New York City, they poignantly note, represent "more than an architectural movement; they were largely the manifestation of a widespread financial phenomenon." Noting that real estate securities in the 1920s were every bit as "toxic as they are now," they went on to conclude:

> The New York skyline is a stark reminder of securitization's ability to connect capital from a speculative public to building ventures. An increased understanding of the early real estate securities market has the

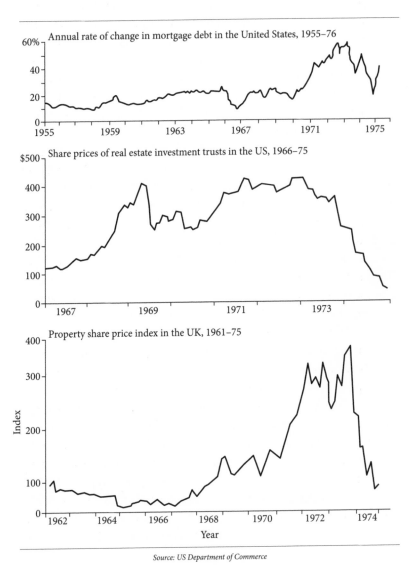

Annual rate of change in mortgage debt in the United States, 1955–76

Share prices of real estate investment trusts in the US, 1966–75

Property share price index in the UK, 1961–75

Index

Year

Source: US Department of Commerce

Figure 1   The Property Market Crash of 1973

potential to provide a valuable input when modeling for worst-case scenarios in the future. Optimism in financial markets has the power to raise steel, but it does not make a building pay.[8]

Clearly, property market booms and busts are inextricably intertwined with speculative financial flows, and these booms and busts have serious consequences for the macroeconomy in general, as well as all manner of externality effects upon resource depletion and environmental degradation. Furthermore, the greater the share of property markets in GDP, the more significant the connection between financing and investment in the built environment becomes as a potential source of macro crises. In the case of developing countries such as Thailand—where housing mortgages, if the World Bank Report is right, are equivalent to only 10 percent of GDP—a property crash could certainly contribute to, but not likely totally power, a macroeconomic collapse (of the sort that occurred in 1997–98), whereas in the United States, where housing mortgage debt is equivalent to 40 percent of GDP, it most certainly could and did generate a crisis in 2007–09.

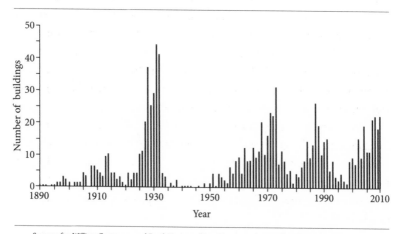

Source: after William Goetzmann and Frank Newman, "Securitization in the 1920s," NBER Working Paper 15650

Figure 2   Tall Buildings Constructed in New York City, 1890–2010

THE MARXIST PERSPECTIVE

Since bourgeois theory, if not totally blind, at best lacks insights in relating urban developments to macroeconomic disruptions, one would have thought that Marxist critics, with their vaunted historical-materialist methods, would have had a field day with fierce denunciations of soaring rents and the savage dispossessions characteristic of what Marx and Engels referred to as the secondary forms of exploitation visited upon the working classes in their living places by merchant capitalists and landlords. They would have set the appropriation of space within the city through gentrification, high-end condo construction, and "Disneyfication" against the barbaric homelessness, lack of affordable housing, and degrading urban environments (both physical, as in air quality, and social, as in crumbling schools and the so-called "benign neglect" of education) for the mass of the population. There has been some of that in a restricted circle of Marxist urbanists and critical theorists (I count myself one).[9] But in fact the structure of thinking within Marxism generally is distressingly similar to that within bourgeois economics. The urbanists are viewed as specialists, while the truly significant core of macroeconomic Marxist theorizing lies elsewhere. Again, the fiction of a national economy takes precedence because that is where the data can most easily be found and, to be fair, where some of the major policy decisions are taken. The role of the property market in creating the crisis conditions of 2007–09, and its aftermath of unemployment and austerity (much of it administered at the local and municipal level), is not well understood, because there has been no serious attempt to integrate an understanding of processes of urbanization and built-environment formation into the general theory of the laws of motion of capital. As a consequence, many Marxist theorists, who love crises to death, tend to treat the recent crash as an obvious manifestation of their favored version of Marxist crisis theory (be it falling rates of profit, underconsumption, or whatever).

Marx is to some degree himself to blame, though unwittingly so, for this state of affairs. In the introduction to the *Grundrisse*, he states that his objective in writing *Capital* is to explicate the general laws of motion of capital. This meant concentrating exclusively on the production and realization of surplus value while abstracting from and excluding what he called the "particularities" of distribution (interest, rents, taxes, and even actual wage and profit rates), since these are accidental, conjunctural and of-the-moment in space and time. He also abstracted from the specificities of exchange relations, such as supply and demand and the state of competition. When demand and supply are in equilibrium, he argued, they cease to explain anything, while the coercive laws of competition function as the enforcer rather than the determinant of the general laws of motion of capital. This immediately provokes the thought of what happens when the enforcement mechanism is lacking, as happens under conditions of monopolization, and what happens when we include spatial competition in our thinking, which is, as has long been known, always a form of monopolistic competition (as in the case of inter-urban competition). Finally, Marx depicts consumption as a "singularity"—those unique instances that together make up a common mode of life—which in being chaotic, unpredictable and uncontrollable, is therefore, in Marx's view, generally outside of the field of political economy (the study of use values, he declares on the first page of *Capital*, is the business of history and not of political economy), and therefore potentially dangerous for capital. Hardt and Negri have therefore recently been at pains to revive this concept, for they see singularities, which both arise from the proliferation of the common and always point back to the common, as a key part of resistance.

Marx also identified another level—that of the metabolic relation to nature, which is a universal condition of all forms of human society and therefore broadly irrelevant to an understanding of the general laws of motion of capital understood as a specific social and historical construct. Environmental issues have a shadowy presence throughout *Capital* for this reason (which does not imply that Marx thought them unimportant or insignificant, any more than he dismissed consumption as irrelevant in the grander scheme of things).[10]

Throughout most of *Capital*, Marx sticks broadly to the framework outlined in the *Grundrisse*. He focuses sharply on the generality of production of surplus value and excludes everything else. He recognizes from time to time that there are problems in so doing. There is, he notes, some "double positing" going on—land, labor, money, and commodities are crucial facts of production, while interest, rents, wages, and profits are excluded from the analysis as particularities of distribution.

The virtue of Marx's approach is that it allows a very clear account of the general laws of motion of capital to be constructed in a way that abstracts from the specific and particular conditions of his time (such as the crises of 1847–48 and 1857–58). This is why we can still read him today in ways that are relevant to our own times. But this approach imposes costs. To begin with, Marx makes clear that the analysis of an actually existing capitalist society/situation requires a dialectical integration of the universal, the general, the particular, and the singular aspects of a society construed as a working, organic totality. We cannot hope, therefore, to explain actual events (such as the crisis of 2007–09) simply in terms of the general laws of motion of capital (this is one of my objections to those who try to cram the facts of the present crisis into some theory of the falling rate of profit). But, conversely, we cannot attempt such an explanation without reference to the general laws of motion (though Marx himself appears to do so in his account in *Capital* of the "independent and autonomous" financial and commercial crisis of 1847–48, or even more dramatically in his historical studies of *The Eighteenth Brumaire* and *Class Struggles in France*, where the general laws of motion of capital are never mentioned).[11]

Secondly, the abstractions within Marx's chosen level of generality start to fracture as the argument in *Capital* progresses. There are many examples of this, but the one that is most conspicuous, and in any case most germane to the argument here, relates to Marx's handling of the credit system. Several times in Volume 1 and repeatedly in Volume 2, Marx invokes the credit system only to lay it aside as a fact of distribution that he is not prepared yet to confront. The general laws of motion he studies in Volume 2, particularly those of fixed capital circulation (including investment in the built environment) and working periods, production periods, circulation times, and turnover times, all end up not only invoking but *necessitating* the credit system. He is very explicit on this point. When commenting on how the money capital advanced must always be greater than that applied in surplus-value production in order to deal with differential turnover times, he notes how changes in turnover times can "set free" some of the money earlier advanced. "This money capital that is set free by the mechanism of the turnover movement (together with the money capital set free by the successive reflux of the fixed capital and that needed for variable capital in every labor process) must play a significant role, as soon as the credit system has developed, *and must also form one of the foundations for this*."[12] In this and other similar comments it is made clear that the credit system becomes absolutely necessary for capital circulation, and that some accounting of the credit system has to be incorporated into the general laws of motion of capital. But when we get to the analysis of the credit system in Volume 3, we find that the interest rate (a particularity) is set jointly by supply and demand and by the state of competition—two specificities that have earlier been totally excluded from the theoretical level of generality at which Marx prefers to work.

I mention this because the significance of the rules that Marx imposed upon his inquiries in *Capital* has largely been ignored. When these rules necessarily get not only bent but broken, as happens in the case of credit and interest, then new prospects for theorizing are opened up that go beyond the insights that Marx has already produced. Marx actually recognizes this might happen at the very outset of his endeavors. In the *Grundrisse*, he thus says of consumption, the most recalcitrant of his categories for analysis given the singularities involved, that while it, like the study of use values, "actually belongs outside of economics," the possibility exists for consumption to react "in turn upon the point of departure (production) and initiate the whole process anew."[13] This is particularly the case with productive consumption, the labor process itself. Mario Tronti and those who followed in his footsteps, such as Tony Negri, are therefore perfectly correct to see the labor process as itself constituted as a singularity, internalized within the general laws of motion of capital.[14] The legendary difficulties faced by capitalists as they seek to mobilize the "animal spirits" of the workers to produce surplus value signals the existence of this singularity in the heart of the production process (this is nowhere more obvious than in the construction industry, as we shall soon see). Internalizing the credit system and the relation between the rate of interest and the rate of profit within the general laws of production, circulation, and realization of capital is likewise a disruptive necessity if we are to bring Marx's theoretical apparatus more acutely to bear on actual events.

The integration of credit into the general theory has to be carefully done, however, in ways that preserve, albeit in a transformed state, the theoretical insights already gained. We cannot, for example, treat the credit system simply as an entity in itself, a kind of efflorescence located on Wall Street or in the City of London that floats freely above the grounded activities on Main Street. A lot of credit-based activity may indeed be speculative froth, and a disgusting excrescence of human lust for gold and pure money power. But much of it is fundamental and absolutely necessary to the functioning of capital. The boundaries between what is necessary and what is (a) necessarily fictitious (as in the case of state and mortgage debt) and (b) pure excess, are not easy to define.

Clearly, to try to analyze the dynamics of the recent crisis and its aftermath without reference to the credit system (with mortgages standing at 40 percent of GDP in the United States), consumerism (70 percent of the driving force in the US economy compared to 35 percent in China), and the state of competition (monopoly power in financial, real estate, retailing, and many other markets) would be a ridiculous enterprise. In the United States $1.4 trillion in mortgages, many of them toxic, are sitting on the secondary markets of Fannie Mae and Freddie Mac, thus forcing the government to allocate $400 billion to a potential rescue effort (with around $142 billion already spent). To understand this, we need to unpack what Marx might mean by the category of "fictitious capital" and its connectivity to land and property markets. We need a way to understand how securitization, as Goetzmann and Newman put it, connects "capital from a speculative public to building ventures." For was it not speculation in the values of land and housing prices and rents that played a fundamental role in the formation of this crisis?

Fictitious capital, for Marx, is not a figment of some Wall Street trader's cocaine-addled brain. It is a fetish construct, which means, given Marx's characterization of fetishism in Volume 1 of *Capital*, that it is real enough, but that it is a surface phenomenon that disguises something important about underlying social relations. When a bank lends to the state and receives interest in return, it appears as if there is something directly productive going on within the state that is actually producing value, when most (but not all, as I shall shortly show) of what goes on within the state (like fighting wars) has nothing to do with value production. When the bank lends to a consumer to buy a house and receives a flow of interest in return, it makes it seem as if something is going on in the house that is directly producing value, when that is not the case. When banks take up bond issues to construct hospitals, universities, schools and the like in return for interest, it seems as if value is being produced in those institutions when it is not. When banks lend to purchase land and property in search of extracting rents, then the distributive category of rent becomes absorbed into the flow of fictitious capital circulation.[15] When banks lend to other banks, or when the Central Bank lends to the commercial banks who lend to land speculators looking to appropriate rents, then fictitious capital looks more and more like an infinite regression of fictions built upon fictions. Leveraging at ever higher ratios (lending out thirty as opposed to three times the amount of cash deposits on hand) magnifies the fictional amounts of money capital in circulation. These are all examples of fictitious capital formations and flows. And it is these flows that convert real into unreal estate.

Marx's point is that the interest that is paid comes from value production somewhere else—taxation or direct extractions on surplus-value production, or levies on revenues (wages and profits). And for Marx, of course, the only place where value and surplus value are created is in the labor process of production. What goes on in fictitious capital circulation may be socially necessary to sustaining capitalism. It may be part of the necessary costs of production and reproduction. Secondary forms of surplus value can be extracted by capitalist enterprises through the exploitation of workers employed by retailers, banks and hedge funds. But Marx's point is that, if there is no value and surplus value being produced in production in general, then these sectors cannot exist by themselves. If no shirts and shoes were produced, what would retailers sell?

There is, however, a caveat that is terribly important. Some of the flow of what seems to be fictitious capital can indeed be involved in value creation. When I convert my mortgaged house into a sweatshop employing illegal immigrants, the house becomes fixed capital in production. When the state builds roads and other infrastructures that function as collective means of production for capital, these then have to be categorized as "productive state expenditures." When the hospital or university becomes the site for innovation and design of new drugs, equipment, and the like, it becomes a site of production. Marx would not be fazed by these caveats at all. As he says of fixed capital, whether something functions as fixed capital or not depends upon its use and not upon its physical qualities.[16] Fixed capital declines when textile lofts are converted into condominiums, while micro-finance converts peasant huts into (far cheaper) fixed capital of production!

Much of the value and surplus value created in production is siphoned off to pass, by all manner of complicated paths, through fictitious channels. And when banks lend to other banks, even leverage on each other, then it is clear that all manner of both socially unnecessary side-payments and speculative movements become possible, built upon the perpetually shifting terrain of fluctuating asset values. Those asset values depend upon a critical process of "capitalization," which Marx views as a form of fictitious capital formation:

> Any regular periodic income can be capitalized by reckoning it up, on the basis of the average rate of interest as that sum that a capital lent out at this interest rate would yield … For the person who buys this ownership title the annual [money received] does actually represent the conversion of the capital he has invested into interest. In this way, all connection with the actual process of capital's valorization is lost, right down to the last trace, confirming the notion that *capital is automatically valorized by its own powers.*[17]

A revenue stream from some asset, such as land, property, a stock, or whatever, is assigned a capital value at which it can be traded, depending upon the interest and discount rates determined by supply and demand conditions in the money market. How to value such assets when there is no market for them became a huge problem in 2008, and it has not gone away. The question of how toxic the toxic assets held by Fannie Mae really are gives almost everyone a headache. (What is the real value of a foreclosed house for which there is no market?) There is an important echo here of the capital value controversy that erupted and was promptly buried, like all manner of other inconvenient truths, in conventional economic theory in the early 1970s.

The problem that the credit system poses is that it is on the one hand vital to the production, circulation, and realization of capital flows at the same time as it is, on the other hand, the pinnacle of all manner of speculative and other "insane forms." It is this that led Marx to characterize Isaac Péreire—who, along with his brother Émile, was one of the masters of the speculative reconstruction of urban Paris under Haussmann—as having "the nicely mixed character of swindler and prophet."[18]

CAPITAL ACCUMULATION THROUGH URBANIZATION

Urbanization, I have long argued, has been a key means for the absorption of capital and labor surpluses throughout capitalism's history.[19] It has a very particular function in the dynamics of capital accumulation because of the long working periods and turnover times and the long lifetimes of most investments in the built environment. It also has a geographical specificity such that the production of space and of spatial monopolies becomes integral to the dynamics of accumulation, not simply by virtue of the changing patterns of commodity flows over space but also by virtue of the very nature of the created and produced spaces and places over which such movements occur. But precisely because all of this activity—which, by the way, is a hugely important arena for value and surplus-value production—is so long-term, it calls for some combination of finance capital and state engagements as absolutely fundamental to its functioning. This activity is clearly speculative in the long term, and always runs the risk of replicating, at a much later date and on a magnified scale, the very overaccumulation conditions that it initially helps to relieve. Hence the crisis-prone character of urban and other forms of physical infrastructural investments (transcontinental railroads and highways, dams, and the like).

The cyclical character of such investments has been well documented for the nineteenth century in the meticulous work of Brinley Thomas (see Figure 3).[20] But the theory of construction business cycles became neglected after 1945 or so, in part because state-led Keynesian-style interventions were deemed effective in flattening them out. Robert

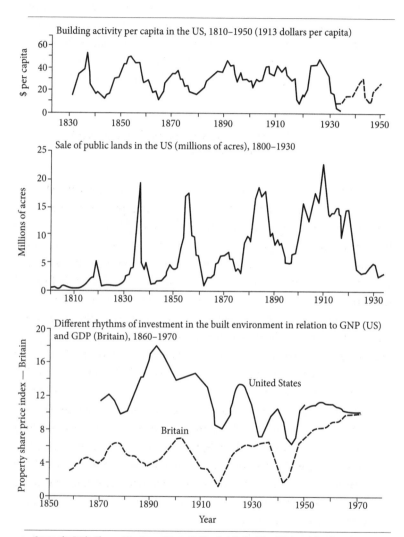

Building activity per capita in the US, 1810–1950 (1913 dollars per capita)

Sale of public lands in the US (millions of acres), 1800–1930

Different rhythms of investment in the built environment in relation to GNP (US) and GDP (Britain), 1860–1970

United States

Britain

Year

Source: after Brinley Thomas, Migration and Economic Growth: A Study of Great Britain and the Atlantic Economy, Cambridge, Cambridge University Press

Figure 3   Long-Run Business Cycles in the US and the UK

Gottlieb, in a detailed study of many local building cycles (published in 1976), identified long swings in residential building cycles, with an average periodicity of 19.7 years and a standard deviation of five years. But his data also suggested that these swings had been dampened, if not eliminated, during the period after World War II.[21] But the abandonment of systemic Keynesian contra-cyclical interventions after the mid 1970s in many parts of the world would suggest that a return to some such cyclical behavior was more than a little likely. This is exactly what we have seen, though I think the case can be made that these swings are more strongly connected to volatile asset bubbles now than was the case in the past (though the NBER accounts of the 1920s might be taken as evidence contrary to that view). These cyclical movements—and this is of equal importance—have also come to exhibit a more complicated geographical configuration. Booms in one place (the US south and west in the 1980s) correspond to crashes somewhere else (the older deindustrializing cities of the midwest of the same period).

Without a general perspective of this sort, we cannot even begin to understand the dynamics that led into the catastrophe of housing markets and urbanization in 2008 in certain regions and cities of the United States, as well as in Spain, Ireland, and the United Kingdom. By the same token, we cannot understand some of the paths that are currently being taken, particularly in China, to get out of the mess that was fundamentally produced elsewhere. For in the same way that Brinley Thomas documents contra-cyclical movements between Britain and the United States in the nineteenth century, such that a boom in residential construction on one side of the Atlantic was balanced by recessions on the other, so we now see stagnation in construction in the United States and much of Europe being counterbalanced by a huge urbanization and infrastructural investment boom centered in China (with several off-shoots elsewhere, particularly in the so-called BRIC countries). And just to get the macro-picture connection right, we should immediately note that the United States and Europe are mired in low growth, while China is registering a 10 percent growth rate (with the other BRIC countries not far behind).

The pressure for the housing market and urban development in the United States to absorb surplus and overaccumulating capital through speculative activity began to build in the mid 1990s, when President Clinton launched his National Partners in Homeownership initiative to confer the supposed benefits of homeownership on lower-income and minority populations. Political pressures were put on respectable financial institutions, including Fannie Mae and Freddie Mac (government-sponsored enterprises holding and marketing mortgages), to lower their lending standards to accommodate this initiative. The mortgage institutions responded with gusto—lending at will, short-circuiting regulatory controls—while their directors reaped huge personal fortunes, all in the name of doing good by helping underprivileged people enjoy the supposed benefits of homeownership. This process fiercely accelerated after the end of the high-tech bubble and the stock market crash of 2001. By then, the housing lobby, led by Fannie Mae, was welded into an autonomous center of ever-growing affluence, influence, and power capable of corrupting everything from Congress and the regulatory agencies to prestigious academic economists (including Joseph Stiglitz), who produced reams of research to show that their activities were very low-risk. The influence of these institutions, coupled with the low interest rates favored by Greenspan at the Fed, unquestionably fueled the boom in housing production and realization.[22] As Goetzmann and Newman remark, finance (backed by the state) can build cities and suburbs, but it cannot necessarily make them pay. So what fueled the demand?

FICTITIOUS CAPITAL AND FICTIONS THAT CANNOT LAST

To understand the dynamics we have to understand how productive and fictitious capital circulation combine within the credit system in the context of property markets. Financial institutions lend to developers, landowners, and construction companies to build, say, suburban tract housing around San Diego, or condos in Florida or southern Spain. The viability of this sector relies on the assumption that value cannot only be produced but also realized in the market. This is where fictitious capital comes in. Money is lent to purchasers who presumably have the ability to pay out of their revenues (wages or profits), which are capitalized as an interest flow on the capital lent out. A flow of fictitious capital is needed to complete the process of the production and realization of housing and commercial property values.

This difference is similar to that between what Marx identifies in *Capital* as "loan capital" for production and the discounting of bills of exchange which facilitates the realization of values in the market.[23] In the cases of housing and condominium construction in, say, Southern California or Florida, the same finance company can furnish the finance to build and the finance to buy what has been built. In some instances the financial institution organizes pre-sales on apartments in condos that have not yet been built. Capital therefore to some degree manipulates and controls both supply and demand for new tract housing and condos as well as for commercial properties (which is totally at odds with the idea of the freely functioning markets that the World Bank Report supposes to be in place).[24]

But the supply–demand relationship is lopsided, because the production and circulation time for housing and commercial properties is very long compared with most other commodities. This is where the disparate production, circulation, and turnover times, which Marx so cannily analyzes in Volume 2 of *Capital*, become crucial. Contracts that finance construction are drawn up long before sales can begin. The time-lags are often substantial. This is particularly true for commercial real estate. The Empire State Building in New York opened on May Day 1931, almost two years after the stock market crash and more than three years after the real estate crash. The twin towers were planned before but opened after the crash of 1973 (and for years could find no private tenants). The downtown rebuilding on the 9/11 site is about to come on line when commercial property values are depressed!

The existing stock of properties that can be traded (some of it of quite ancient origin) is also large relative to what can be produced. Total housing supply is therefore relatively inelastic relative to more volatile demand shifts: historically it has proved very difficult in developed countries to increase the housing stock in any one year by more than 2 or 3 percent even with the greatest effort (though China, as in all things, may break through that constraint).

Stimulating demand by taxation and public policy gimmicks and other incentives (such as increasing the volume of sub-prime mortgages) does not necessarily elicit an increased supply: it merely inflates prices and stimulates speculation. As much if not more money can then be made from financial trading on existing housing rather than from building new. It becomes more profitable to finance shady mortgage-originating institutions like Countrywide than actual housing production. Even more tempting is to invest in collateralized debt obligations made up of tranches of mortgages gathered together in some spuriously highly rated investment vehicle (supposedly "as safe as houses") in which the flow of interest from homeowners provides a steady income (no matter whether the homeowners are creditworthy or not). This was exactly what happened in the United States as the sub-prime steamroller got going. Copious amounts of fictitious capital flowed into housing finance to fuel demand, but only a part of it ended up in new housing production. The sub-prime market for mortgages, which stood at around $30 billion in the mid 1990s, rose to $130 billion by 2000, and hit an all-time high of $625 billion in 2005.[25] There was no way that such a rapid increase in demand could be paralleled by an expansion of supply, no matter how hard the builders tried. So prices rose, and it seemed like they could rise forever.

But this all depended on a continuous expansion of the flows of ficti-tious capital, and on keeping intact the fetish belief that capital can be "automatically valorized by its own powers."[26] Marx's point, of course, is that, in the face of an insufficiency of value-creation through production, that fantasy must inevitably come to a sticky end. And indeed it did.

The class interests involved on the production side are, however, also lopsided, and this has implications for who ends up holding the "sticky end." Bankers, developers, and construction companies easily combine to forge a class alliance (one that often dominates what is called "the urban growth machine" both politically and economically[27]). But con-sumer housing mortgages are singular and dispersed, and often involve loans to those who occupy a different class or, particularly in the United States (though not in Ireland), racial or ethnic position. With securitiza-tion of mortgages, the finance company could simply pass any risk on to someone else (for example, Fannie Mae, which was eager to procure such risk as part of its growth strategy)—which is precisely what they did, after having creamed off all the origination and legal fees that they could. If the financier has to choose between the bankruptcy of a developer because of failures of realization or the bankruptcy and foreclosure on the purchaser of housing (particularly if the purchaser is from the lower classes or from a racial or ethnic minority and the mortgage has already been passed on to someone else), then it is fairly clear which way the financial system will lean. Class and racial prejudices are invariably involved.

Speculatively, the asset markets constituted by housing and land have a Ponzi character without a Bernie Madoff at the top. I buy a property, the property prices go up, and a rising market encourages others to buy. When the pool of truly creditworthy buyers dries up, then why not go further down the income layers to higher-risk consumers, ending up with no-income and no-asset buyers who might gain by flipping the property as prices rise? And so it goes until the bubble pops. Financial institutions have tremendous incentives to sustain the bubble as long as they can in order to extract maximum fees. The problem is that they often can't get off the train before it wrecks, because the train is accelerating so quickly. The delusion that capital can "valorize itself by way of its own powers" is self-perpetuating and self-fulfilling, at least for a while. As one of Michael Lewis's perceptive financial analysts who saw the crash coming early on put it in *The Big Short*: "Holy shit, this isn't just credit. This is a fictitious Ponzi scheme."[28]

There is yet another wrinkle to this story. Rising housing prices in the US increased effective demand in the economy at large. In the year 2003 alone, 13.6 million mortgages were issued (as opposed to less than half that ten years before), worth $3.7 trillion. Of these, $2.8 trillion's worth were for purposes of refinancing (for comparison, the total US GDP at that time was less than $15 trillion). Households were cashing in on the rising value of their property. With wages stagnant, this provided a way for many to access extra cash either for necessities (like health care) or consumer goods (a new car or vacation). The house became a convenient cash cow, a personal ATM machine, thus boosting aggregate demand, including, of course, the further demand for housing. Michael Lewis in *The Big Short* explains the sort of thing that happened. The baby nurse of one of his lead characters ended up owning, with her sister, six houses in Queens in New York City. "After they bought the first one, and its value rose, the lenders came and suggested they refinance and take out $250,000—which they used to buy another." Then the price of that one rose, too, and they repeated the experiment. "By the time they were done they owned five of them and the market was falling and they couldn't make any of the payments."[29] Property prices can't and don't rise forever.

THE PRODUCTION OF VALUE AND URBAN CRISES

But there are longer-term and deeper issues here that need to be taken into account on the production side. Although much of what went into the real estate market was pure speculation, the production activity was itself an important part of the economy as a whole, with construction accounting for 7 percent of GDP, and all of the ancillaries of new products (from furnishings to cars) amounting to more than double that. If the NBER papers are correct, the collapse of the construction boom after 1928, which was manifest as a $2 billion drop-off (huge for the time) in housing construction and a collapse of housing starts to less than 10 percent of their former volume in the larger cities, played an important but still not well-understood role in the 1929 crash. A Wikipedia entry notes: "devastating was the disappearance of 2 million high paying jobs in the construction trades, plus the loss of profits and rents that humbled many landlords and real estate investors."[30] This surely had implications for confidence in the stock market more generally.

Small wonder that there were desperate subsequent attempts by the Roosevelt administration back in the 1930s to revive the housing sector. To that end a raft of reforms in housing mortgage finance were implemented, culminating in the creation of a secondary mortgage market through the founding in 1938 of the Federal National Mortgage Association (Fannie Mae). The task of Fannie Mae was to insure mortgages and to allow banks and other lenders to pass the mortgages on, thus providing much-needed liquidity to the housing market. These institutional reforms were later to play a vital role in financing the suburbanization of the United States after World War II. While necessary, they were not, however, sufficient to put housing construction onto a different plane in US economic development. All sorts of tax incentives (such as the mortgage interest tax deduction), along with the GI Bill and a very positive housing act of 1947, which declared the right of all Americans to live in "decent housing in a decent living environment," were devised to promote homeownership, for political as well as economic reasons. Homeownership was widely promoted as central to the "American Dream," and it rose from just above 40 percent of the population in the 1940s to more than 60 percent by the 1960s, and close to 70 percent at its peak in 2004 (as of 2010, it had fallen to 66 percent). Homeownership may be a deeply held cultural value in the United States, but cultural values flourish remarkably when promoted and subsidized by state policies. The stated reasons for such policies are all those that the World Bank Report cites. But the political reason is rarely now acknowledged. As was openly noted in the 1930s, debt-encumbered homeowners do not go on strike.[31] The military personnel returning from service in World War II would have constituted a social and political threat had they returned to unemployment and depression. What better way to kill two birds with one stone: revive the economy through massive housing construction and suburbanization and co-opt the better-paid workers into conservative politics by debt-encumbered homeownership! Furthermore, boosting demand by public policies led to steady increases in the asset values of homeowners, which was great for them but a disaster from the standpoint of the rational use of land and space.

During the 1950s and 1960s these policies worked, both from the political and the macroeconomic viewpoints, since they underpinned two decades of very strong growth in the United States, the effects of which spilled over globally. Housing construction shifted onto another plane entirely in relation to economic growth (see Figure 4). "It is a long-standing pattern," writes Binyamin Appelbaum, "that Americans recover from recessions by building more homes and filling them with things."[32] The problem back in the 1960s was that the sprawling urbanization process was dynamic, but both environmentally unsustainable and geographically uneven. The unevenness largely reflected the differentiated income streams that flowed to different segments of the working class. While the suburbs thrived, the inner cities stagnated and declined. The white working class flourished, but the impacted inner city minorities —African-American in particular—did not. The result was a whole

sequence of inner-city uprisings—including Detroit and Watts, and culminating in spontaneous uprisings in some forty cities across the United
States in the wake of the assassination of Martin Luther King in 1968.
Something that came to be known as "the urban crisis" was there for all
to see and easily name (even though it was not, strictly speaking, a macroeconomic crisis of urbanization). Massive federal funds were released
to deal with this problem after 1968, until President Nixon declared the
crisis over (for fiscal reasons) in the recession of 1973.[33]

The side-bar to all of this was that Fannie Mae became a government-
sponsored private enterprise in 1968 and, after it was provided with a
"competitor," the Federal Home Mortgage Corporation (Freddie Mac)
in 1970, both institutions played a hugely important and eventually
destructive role in promoting homeownership and sustaining housing
construction over nearly fifty years. Home mortgage debt now accounts
for some 40 percent of the accumulated private debt of the United States,
much of which, as we have seen, is toxic. And both Fannie Mae and
Freddie Mac have passed back into government control. What to do
about them is an intensely debated political question (as are the subsidies
to homeownership demand) in relation to US indebtedness more generally. Whatever happens will have major consequences for the future of
the housing sector in particular and urbanization more generally in relation to capital accumulation within the United States.

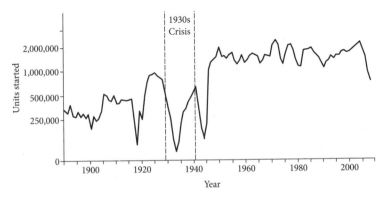

Figure 4   Housing Starts in the United States,1890–2008

The current signs in the United States are not encouraging. The housing sector is not reviving, and new housing production is depressed and stagnant. There are signs it is heading for a dreaded "double-dip" recession, as Federal monies dry up and unemployment remains high. Housing starts have plunged for the first time to below pre-1940s levels (see Figure 4). As of March 2011, the unemployment rate in construction stood above 20 percent, compared to a rate of 9.7 percent in manufacturing that was very close to the national average. There is no need to build new homes and fill them with things when so many homes stand empty. The San Francisco Federal Reserve "estimates construction may not return to the average level of pre-bubble activity before 2016, sidelining a major industry" from having any impact on the recovery.[34] In the Great Depression, more than a quarter of construction workers remained unemployed as late as 1939. Getting them back to work was a crucial target for public interventions (such as the WPA). Attempts by the Obama administration to create a stimulus package for infrastructural investments have largely been frustrated by Republican opposition. To make matters worse, the condition of state and local finances in the US is so dire as to result in layoffs and furloughs, as well as savage cuts in urban services. The collapse of the housing market and the 20 percent fall in housing prices has put a huge dent in local finances, which rely heavily on property taxes. An urban fiscal crisis is brewing as state and municipal governments cut back and construction languishes. When we put this all together, it looks increasingly as if the post–World War II era of accumulation and macroeconomic stabilization by suburbanization and housing and property development in the United States is at an end.

On top of all this comes a class politics of austerity that is being pursued for political and not economic reasons. Radical right-wing Republican administrations at the state and local levels are using the so-called debt crisis to savage government programs and reduce state and local government employment. This has, of course, been a long-standing tactic of a capital-inspired assault on government programs more generally. Reagan cut taxes on the wealthy from 72 percent to around 30 percent and launched a debt-financed arms race with the Soviet Union. The debt soared under Reagan as a result. As his budget director David Stockman later noted, running up the debt became a convenient excuse to go after government regulation (for example, on the environment) and social programs, in effect externalizing the costs of environmental degradation and social reproduction. President Bush Jnr faithfully followed suit, with his Vice-President Dick Cheney proclaiming that "Reagan taught us that deficits do not matter."[35] Tax cuts for the rich, two unfunded wars in Iraq and Afghanistan, and a huge gift to big pharma through a state-funded prescription drug program, turned what had been a budget surplus under Clinton into a sea of red ink, enabling the Republican party and conservative democrats later to do big capital's bidding, and go as far as possible in externalizing those costs that capital never wants to bear: the costs of environmental degradation and social reproduction. The assault on the environment and the well-being of the people is palpable, and in the US and much of Europe it is taking place for political and class, not economic reasons. It is inducing, as David Stockman has very recently noted, a state of plain class war. As Warren Buffett also put it, "sure there is class war, and it is my class, the rich, who are making it and we are winning."[36] The only question is: When will the people start to wage class war back? And one of the places to start would be to focus on the rapidly degrading qualities of urban life, through foreclosures, the persistence of predatory practices in urban housing markets, reductions in services, and above all the lack of viable employment opportunities in urban labor markets almost everywhere, with some cities (Detroit being the sad poster child) utterly bereft of employment prospects. The crisis now is as much an urban crisis as it ever was.

PREDATORY URBAN PRACTICES

In *The Communist Manifesto*, Marx and Engels note in passing that, no sooner does the worker receive "his wages in cash, than he is set upon by the other portions of the bourgeoisie, the landlord, the shopkeeper, the pawnbroker, etc."[37] Marxists have traditionally relegated such forms of exploitation, and the class struggles (for such they are) that inevitably arise around them, to the shadows of their theorizing, as well as to the margins of their politics. But I want to argue here that they constitute, at least in the advanced capitalist economies, a vast terrain of accumulation by dispossession, through which money is sucked up into the circulation of fictitious capital to underpin the vast fortunes made from within the financial system.

The predatory practices that were omnipresent before the crash in the housing market in general and within the sub-prime lending field in particular were legendary in their proportions. Before the main crisis broke, the low-income African-American population of the United States was already estimated to have lost somewhere between $71 and $93 billion in asset values through predatory sub-prime practices.[38] The dispossessions came in two waves—one mini-wave between the announcement of the Clinton initiative of 1995 and the collapse of Long Term Capital Management in 1998, and the other after 2001. Contemporaneously with the latter period, the bonuses on Wall Street and the earnings in the mortgage-initiating industry were soaring, with unheard-of profit rates from pure financial manipulations, particularly those associated with the securitization of high-cost but risky mortgages. The inference is that, by various hidden channels, massive transfers of wealth from the poor to the rich were occurring, beyond those since documented in the plainly shady and often illegal practices of mortgage companies like Countrywide, through financial manipulations in housing markets.[39]

What has happened since the crash is even more astonishing. Many of the foreclosures (over a million during 2010) turn out to have been illegal, if not downright fraudulent, leading a congressman from Florida to write to the Florida Supreme Court Justice that "if the reports I am hearing are true, the illegal foreclosures taking place represent the largest seizure of private property ever attempted by banks and government entities."[40] The attorney generals in all fifty states are now investigating the problem, but (as might be expected) most seem anxious to close out the investigations in as summary a way as possible at the price of a few financial settlements (but no restitutions of illegally seized properties). Certainly, no one is likely to go to jail for it, even though there is clear evidence of systematic forgery of legal documents.

Predatory practices of this sort have been long-standing. So let me give some instances from Baltimore. Shortly after arriving in the city in 1969, I became involved in a study of inner-city housing provision that focused on the role of different actors—landlords, tenants and homeowners, the brokers and lenders, the FHA, the city authorities (Housing Code Enforcement in particular)—in the production of the terrifying rat-infested inner-city living conditions in the areas wracked by uprisings in the wake of the assassination of Martin Luther King. The vestiges of red-lining of areas of low-income African-American populations denied credit were etched into the map of the city, but exclusions were by then justified as a legitimate response to high credit risk, and not supposedly to race. In several areas of the city, active blockbusting practices were to be found. This generated high profits for ruthless real estate companies. But for this to work, African-Americans had also somehow to acquire access to mortgage finance when they were all lumped together as a high-credit-risk population. This could be done by way of something called the "Land Installment Contract." In effect, African-Americans were "helped" by property owners who acted as an intermediary to the credit markets and took out a mortgage in their own names. After a few years, when some of the principle plus the interest had been paid down, thus proving the family's creditworthiness, the title was supposed to be passed on to the resident, with help from the friendly property owner and local mortgage institution. Some takers made it (though usually in neighborhoods that were declining in value), but in unscrupulous hands (and there were many in Baltimore—though apparently not so many in Chicago, where this system was also common) this could be a particularly predatory form of accumulation by dispossession.[41] The property owner was permitted to charge fees to cover property taxes, administrative and legal costs, and the like. These fees (sometimes exorbitant) could be added to the principal of the mortgage. After years of steady payment, many families found they owed more on the principal on the house than they had at the start. If they failed once to pay the higher payments after interest rates rose, the contract was voided and families were evicted. Such practices caused something of a scandal. A Civil Rights action was started against the worst landlord offenders. But it failed, because those who had signed on to the land installment contract had simply failed to read the small print, or to have their own lawyer (which poor people rarely have) to read it for them (the small print is in any case incomprehensible to ordinary mortals—have you ever read the small print on your credit card?).

Predatory practices of this sort never went away. The land-installment contract was displaced by practices of "flipping" in the 1980s (a property dealer would buy a run-down house cheaply, put in a few cosmetic repairs—much overvalued—and arrange "favorable" mortgage finance for the unsuspecting buyer, who lived in the house only so long as the roof did not fall in or the furnace blow up). And when the sub-prime market began to form in the 1990s in response to the Clinton initiative, cities like Baltimore, Cleveland, Detroit, Buffalo, and the like became major centers for a growing wave of accumulation by dispossession ($70 billion or more nation-wide). Baltimore eventually launched a Civil Rights lawsuit after the crash of 2008 against Wells Fargo over its discriminatory sub-prime lending practices (reverse red-lining in which people were steered into taking sub-prime rather than conventional loans, in which African-Americans and single-headed households—headed by women—were systematically exploited). Almost certainly the suit will fail (although at the third iteration it has been allowed to go forward in the courts), since it will be almost impossible to prove intent based on race as opposed to credit risk. As usual, the incomprehensible small print allows for a lot (consumers beware!). Cleveland took a more nuanced path: sue the finance companies for the creation of a public nuisance because the landscape was littered with foreclosed houses that required city action to board them up!

Predatory practices that hit the poor, the vulnerable, and the already underprivileged are legion. Any small unpaid bill (a license fee or water bill, for example) can become a lien on a property about which a property owner may remain mysteriously (and illegally) unnotified until after it has been bought up by a lawyer who expenses it so that an original unpaid bill of, say, $100 requires, say, $2,500 to redeem. For most poor people, this means the loss of the property. At the last round of lien sales in Baltimore, some $6 million worth of liens on property were purchased from the city by a small group of lawyers. If the markup is 250 percent, they stand to amass considerable fortunes if the liens get paid off, and potentially valuable properties for future development if they simply acquire the properties.

To top it all, it has been systematically shown that, in US cities since the 1960s, the poor typically pay more for inferior basic commodities such as food, and that the under-servicing of low-income communities places added undue financial and practical burdens upon such populations. The economy of dispossession of vulnerable populations is as active as it is perpetual. Even more startling is how many temporary and insecure workers in low-wage industries in major cities such as New York, Chicago, and Los Angeles have experienced some degree of illegal wage losses; including failure to pay the minimum wage, refusal to pay for overtime, or simply delays in payment that could in some instances stretch into months.[42]

My point in mentioning all these various forms of exploitation and dispossession is to suggest that in many metropolitan regions such mass practices are systematically visited upon vulnerable populations. It is important to recognize how easily real wage concessions to workers can be clawed back for the capitalist class as a whole through predatory and exploitative activities in the realm of consumption. For much of the low-income urbanized population, the joint excessive exploitation of their labor and the dispossession of their meager assets constitutes a perpetual drain upon their capacity to sustain minimally adequate conditions of social reproduction. This is a condition that calls for city-wide organization and a city-wide political response (see below).

THE CHINA STORY

In so far as there has been any exit from the global crisis of capital this time, it is notable that the housing and property boom in China, along with a huge wave of debt-financed infrastructural investments there, has taken a leading role not only in stimulating their internal market (and mopping up unemployment in the export industries) but also in stimulating the economies that are tightly integrated into the China trade, such as Australia and Chile with their raw materials and Germany with its machine tool and automotive exports. In the United States, on the other hand, construction has been slow to revive, with the unemployment rate in construction, as noted earlier, more than twice the national average.

Urban investments typically take a long time to produce and an even longer time to mature. It is always difficult to determine, therefore, when an overaccumulation of capital has been or is about to be transformed into an overaccumulation of investments in the built environment. The likelihood of overshooting, as regularly happened with the railways in the nineteenth century and as is shown by the long history of building cycles and crashes (including the debacle of 2007–09), is very high.

The fearlessness of the pell-mell urbanization and infrastructural investment boom that is completely reconfiguring the geography of the Chinese national space rests in part on the ability of the central government to intervene arbitrarily in the banking system if anything goes wrong. A relatively mild recession in property markets in the late 1990s in leading cities such as Shanghai left the banks holding title to a vast array of "non-earning assets" ("toxic," we call them), many of which were urban and property-development based. Unofficial estimates identified as many as 40 percent of bank loans a non-earning.[43] The response of the central government was to use its abundant foreign exchange reserves to re-capitalize the banks (a Chinese version of what later became known as the controversial Troubled Asset Relief Program—TARP—in the United States). It is known that the state used some $45 billion of its foreign exchange reserves for this purpose in the late 1990s, and it may have indirectly used much more. But as China's institutions evolve in ways more consistent with global financial markets, so it becomes harder for the central government to control what is happening in the financial sector.

The reports now available from China make it seem rather too similar for comfort to the American southwest and Florida in the 2000s, or Florida in the 1920s. Since the general privatization of housing in China in 1998, housing speculation and construction have taken off in a spectacular fashion. Housing prices are reported to have risen by 140 percent nationwide since 2007, and by as much as 800 percent in the main cities such as Beijing and Shanghai over the last five years. In the latter city, property prices are reputed to have doubled over the last year alone. The average apartment price there now stands at $500,000 (in a country where per capita GDP was $7,518 in 2010), and even in second-tier cities a typical home "costs about 25 times the average income of residents," which is clearly unsustainable. All of this indicates that housing and commercial property construction, fast and vast as it is, is not keeping pace with actual and, even more importantly, anticipated effective demand.[44] One consequence is the emergence of strong inflationary pressures that have prompted the central government to use a variety of tools to restrict out-of-control local government spending.

The central government openly states its worry that

> too much of the country's growth continues to be tied to inflationary spending on real estate development and government investment in roads, railways and other multibillion dollar infrastructure projects. In the first quarter of 2011, fixed asset investment—a broad measure of building activity—jumped 25 percent from the period a year earlier, and real estate investment soared 37 percent.[45]

This investment "is now equal to nearly 70 percent of the nation's gross domestic product." No other nation has approached this level in modern times. "Even Japan, at the peak of its building boom in the 1980s, reached only about 35 percent, and the figure has hovered around 20 percent for decades in the United States."

The "cities' efforts have helped government infrastructure and real estate spending surpass foreign trade as the biggest contributor to China's growth."[46] Extensive land acquisitions and displacements of legendary proportions in some of the major cities (as many as 3 million people displaced in Beijing over the last ten years) indicate an active economy of dispossession booming alongside this huge urbanization push throughout the whole of China. The forced displacements and dispossessions are one of the most important causes of a rising tide of popular and sometimes violent protests.

The land sales to developers have provided a lucrative cash cow to fill local government coffers. But in early 2011 the central government ordered them to be curbed in order to hold back an out-of-control property market, and the often brutally staged land dispossessions that were causing so much resistance. This created fiscal difficulties for many municipalities. The "sharp rise in local government debt and poor controls over borrowing by investment companies" (many sponsored by local governments) are now considered a major risk to the Chinese economy, and this is casting a deep shadow over the prospects for future growth, not only in China but also worldwide. As of 2011, the municipal debt was estimated by the Chinese government at around $2.2 trillion, equivalent to "nearly a third of the nation's gross domestic product." Possibly as much at 80 percent of this debt is held by off-the-books investment companies, sponsored by but not technically a part of municipal government. These are the organizations that are building, at immense speed, both the new infrastructures and the signature buildings that make Chinese cities so spectacular. But the cumulative debt liabilities of the municipalities are huge. A wave of defaults "could become a huge liability for the central government, which is sitting on about $2 trillion in debt of its own."[47] The possibility of a collapse followed by a long period of "Japanese-like stagnation" is very real. The slowing of the Chinese economic growth machine in 2011 is already producing reductions in imports, and this will in turn rebound in all those areas of the world that have flourished on the back of the Chinese market for raw materials in particular.

Meanwhile, whole new cities, with hardly any residents or real activities as yet, can now be found in the Chinese interior, prompting a curious advertising program in the United States business press to attract investors and companies to this new urban frontier of global capitalism.[48] Urban development since the mid nineteenth century, if not before, has always been speculative, but the speculative scale of Chinese development seems to be of an entirely different order than anything before in human history. But then the surplus liquidity in the global economy needing to be absorbed, which is expanding at a compound rate, has never been greater either.

As in the post–World War II suburbanization boom in the United States, when all the ancillary housing appliances and appurtenances are added in it becomes clear that the Chinese urbanization boom is playing a central role in stimulating the revival of global economic growth for a wide range of consumer goods other than automobiles (in which China now boasts the largest market in the world). "By some estimates, China consumes up to 50 percent of key global commodities and materials such as cement, steel and coal, and Chinese real estate is the main driver of that demand."[49] Since at least half of the steel consumed ends up in the built environment, this means that a quarter of global steel output is now absorbed by this activity alone. China is not the only place where such a property boom can be identified. All of the so-called BRIC countries seem to be following suit. Property prices thus doubled in both São Paulo and Rio last year, and in India and Russia similar conditions prevail. But all of these countries, it should be noted, are experiencing high aggregate growth rates along with strong currents of inflation. Strong urbanization currents clearly have much to do with the rapid recovery from the effects of the recession of 2007–09.

The question is: How sustainable is this recovery, given its roots in largely speculative urban developments? Attempts by the Chinese central government to control their boom and quell inflationary pressures by raising step-wise the reserve requirements of the banks have not been too successful. A "shadow-banking system" has emerged that is strongly connected to land and property investments and is hard to monitor and control, and comprises new investment vehicles (analogous to those that emerged in the 1990s in the US and Britain). The result of accelerating land dispossessions and inflation has been proliferating unrest. Reports are now coming in of work actions by taxi drivers and truckers (in Shanghai), alongside sudden full-blown factory strikes in the industrial areas of Guangdong in response to low wages, poor working conditions, and escalating prices. Official reports of unrest have risen dramatically, and wage adjustments have been occurring, along with government policies designed to confront the swelling unrest and stimulate the internal market as a substitute for riskier and stagnant export markets (Chinese consumerism currently accounts for only 35 percent of GDP, as opposed to 70 percent in the United States).

All of this has to be understood, however, against the background of the concrete steps the Chinese government took to deal with the crisis of 2007–09. The main impact of the crisis on China was the sudden collapse of export markets (particularly that of the United States) and a 20 percent fall-off in exports by early 2009. Several reasonably reliable estimates put the number of jobs lost in the export sector at close to 30 million over a very short period in 2008–09. Yet the IMF could report that the net job loss in China as of fall 2009 was only 3 million.[50] Some of the difference between gross and net job losses may have been due to the return of unemployed urban migrants to their rural base. Another part of it was doubtless the fast revival of exports and re-engagement of workers earlier laid off. But the rest of it was almost certainly due to the government's implementation of a massive Keynesian-style stimulus program of urban and infrastructural investment. An extra $600 billion was made available by the central government to augment what was already a large program of infrastructural investment (a cumulative total of $750 billion allocated solely to build 8,100 miles of high-speed and 11,000 miles of traditional rail, though these investments are now in trouble after a high-speed rail crash that suggests poor design, if not corruption in construction).[51] The central government simultaneously instructed the banks to lend extensively to all manner of local development projects (including the property and infrastructure sectors) as a way to mop up surplus labor. This massive program was designed to lead the way towards economic recovery. The Chinese government now claims it created nearly 34 million new urban jobs between 2008 and 2010. It certainly appears to have been fairly successful in its immediate objective of absorbing much of the massive labor surplus, if the IMF figures on net job loss are correct.

The big question, of course, is whether these state expenditures fall within the category of "productive" or not—and, if so, productive of what and for whom? Many investments, such as the huge shopping mall close to Dongguan, stand almost empty, as do quite a few of the high-rises that litter the urban landscape almost everywhere. And then there are the empty new cities waiting for populations and industries to arrive. Yet there is also no question that the Chinese national space could benefit from deeper and more efficient spatial integration, and on the surface at least the vast wave of infrastructural investments and urbanization projects would appear to do just that, linking the underdeveloped interior to the wealthier coastal regions and the water-short north with the well-watered south. At the metropolitan level, the processes of urban growth and urban regeneration would also appear to bring modernist techniques to urbanization, along with a diversification of activities (including all the mandatory cultural and knowledge industry institutions, exemplified by the spectacular Shanghai Expo, that are so characteristic of neoliberal urbanization in the United States and Europe).

In some ways, China's development mimics and exaggerates that of the post–World War II United States. During those years, the interstate highway system integrated the American South and the West, and this, coupled with suburbanization, then played a crucial role in sustaining both employment and capital accumulation. But the parallel is instructive in other ways. US development after 1945 was not only profligate in its use of energy and land; it also generated, as we have seen, a distinctive crisis for marginalized, excluded and rebellious urban populations, which elicited a raft of policy responses during the late 1960s. All of this faded after the crash of 1973, when President Nixon declared in his State of the Union address that the urban crisis was over and that federal funding would be withdrawn. The effect at the municipal level was to create a crisis in urban services, with all of the terrifying consequences of degeneration in public schooling, public health, and availability of affordable housing from the late 1970s onwards in the United States.

The accelerated urban and infrastructural investment strategy in China is collapsing these two tendencies into a few years. A high-speed train between Shanghai and Beijing is fine for the businesspeople and the upper middle class, but it does not constitute the kind of affordable transport system that can take workers back to their rural origins for the Chinese New Year. Similarly, high-rise apartment blocks, gated communities, and golf courses for the rich, along with high-end shopping malls, do not really help to reconstitute an adequate daily life for the restive, impoverished masses. This lopsidedness in urban development along class lines is in fact a global issue. It is currently arising in India, as well as in the innumerable cities around the world where there are emergent concentrations of marginalized populations alongside high-modernist urbanization and consumerism for an increasingly affluent minority. The issue of how to deal with the impoverished, insecure, and excluded workers that now constitute a majoritarian and putatively dominant power block in many cities is becoming a major political problem. Military planning is, as a result, now highly focused on how to deal with restive and potentially revolutionary urban-based movements.

But in the Chinese case there is one interesting wrinkle to this narrative. The trajectory of development since liberalization began in 1979 rested on the notion that decentralization is one of the best ways to exercise centralized control. The idea was to liberate regional and municipal governments, and even villages and townships, to seek their own

betterment within a framework of centralized control and market coordinations. Successful solutions arrived at through local initiatives then became the basis for the reformulation of central government policies.

Reports emanating from China suggest that the power-transition anticipated for 2012 is faced with an intriguing choice. Attention is focused on the city of Chongqing, where a purportedly radical shift away from market-based policies back onto a path of state-led socialist redistribution—backed, interestingly, by a great deal of Maoist-inspired rhetoric—has been underway for some time. In this model, "everything links back to the issue of poverty and inequality." The government "has turned the market profits of state-owned enterprises toward traditional socialist projects, using their revenues to fund the construction of affordable housing and transportation infrastructure." The housing initiative entails a "massive construction program" to "provide cheap apartments to a third of the 30 million residents" living in the city region. "The municipality expects to build 20 satellite towns, with a population of 300,000 apiece. In each one, 50,000 people will live in state-subsidized housing." The aim of this enormously ambitious project (contrary to World Bank advice) is to reduce the spiraling social inequalities that have arisen over the last two decades across China. It is an antidote to the private developer–led projects of gated communities for the rich. But its downside is that it accelerates the dispossession of land from rural uses and pushes peasant populations into a forced urbanization that underpins swelling protest and discontent, which in turn leads to a repressive if not authoritarian response.

This turn back to a socialist redistributive agenda, using the private sector for public purposes, is now providing a model for the central government to follow. It plans to build 36 million affordable housing units over the five years beginning in 2010. In this way China proposes to solve the capital surplus absorption problem at the same time as offering a way to further urbanize the rural population, absorb surplus labor, and (hopefully) dispel popular discontent by offering reasonable housing security to the less well-off.[52] There are echoes here of US urban policies after 1945: keep economic growth on track while co-opting potentially restive populations through housing security. The downside is the swelling and sometimes violent opposition to the necessary land acquisitions (though the Chinese clearly cling to the Maoist slogan that "you cannot make an omelet without breaking eggs").

But rival market-based developmental models exist elsewhere in China, particularly in the coastal and southern cities, such as Shenzhen. Here the proposed solution is very different. Emphasis is more upon political liberalization and what sounds like more bourgeois urban democracy, alongside a deepening of free market initiatives. In this case, rising social inequality is accepted as a necessary cost of sustained economic growth and competitiveness. Which way the central government will lean is impossible at this point to predict. The key point is the role of urban-based initiatives in pioneering the way towards such choices of different futures; but the means to achieve that future seem to be firmly embedded in a polarized choice between state and market.

The effects of China's urbanization in recent decades have been simply phenomenal and world-shaking in their implications. The absorption of surplus liquidity and overaccumulated capital in urbanization at a time when profitable opportunities are otherwise hard to come by has certainly sustained capital accumulation not only in China but around much of the rest of the globe over the last few crisis years. How stable such a solution might be is open to question. The burgeoning social inequalities (China is now third in the number of billionaires in the world), the environmental degradation (which even the Chinese government openly admits), along with multiple signs of overextensions and overvaluation of assets in the built environment, suggest that the Chinese "model" is far from trouble-free, and that it could all too easily morph overnight from benefactor to problem child of capitalist development. If this "model" fails, then the future of capitalism is dire indeed. This would then imply that the only path open is to look more creatively to the option of exploring anti-capitalist alternatives. If the capitalist form of urbanization is so completely embedded in and foundational for the reproduction of capitalism, then it also follows that alternative forms of urbanization must necessarily become central to any pursuit of an anti-capitalist alternative.

THE URBANIZATION OF CAPITAL

The reproduction of capital passes through processes of urbanization in myriad ways. But the urbanization of capital presupposes the capacity of capitalist class powers to dominate the urban process. This implies capitalist class domination not only over state apparatuses (in particular those aspects of state power that administer and govern the social and infrastructural conditions within territorial structures), but also over whole populations—their lifestyles as well as their labor power, their cultural and political values as well as their mental conceptions of the world. That level of control does not come easily, if at all. The city and the urban process that produces it are therefore major sites of political, social, and class struggles. We have heretofore examined the dynamics of this struggle from the standpoint of capital. It therefore remains to examine the urban process—its disciplinary apparatuses and restraints as well as its emancipatory and anti-capitalist possibilities—from the standpoint of all those who attempt to gain their livelihood and reproduce their daily lives in the midst of this urban process.

CHAPTER THREE

The Creation of the Urban Commons

The city is the site where people of all sorts and classes mingle, however reluctantly and agonistically, to produce a common if perpetually changing and transitory life. The commonality of that life has long been a matter of commentary by urbanists of all stripes, and the compelling subject of a wide range of evocative writings and representations (in novels, films, painting, videos, and the like) that attempt to pin down the character of that life (or the particular character of life in a particular city in a given place and time) and its deeper meanings. And in the long history of urban utopianism, we have a record of all manner of human aspirations to make the city in a different image, more "after our heart's desire" as Park would put it. The recent revival of emphasis upon the supposed loss of urban commonalities reflects the seemingly profound impacts of the recent wave of privatizations, enclosures, spatial controls, policing, and surveillance upon the qualities of urban life in general, and in particular upon the potentiality to build or inhibit new forms of social relations (a new commons) within an urban process influenced if not dominated by capitalist class interests. When Hardt and Negri, for example, argue that we should view "the metropolis as a factory for the production of the common," they suggest this as an entry point for anti-capitalist critique and political activism. Like the right to the city, the idea sounds catchy and intriguing, but what could it possibly mean? And how does this relate to the long history of arguments and debates concerning the creation and utilization of common property resources?

I have lost count of the number of times I have seen Garrett Hardin's classic article on "The Tragedy of the Commons" cited as an irrefutable argument for the superior efficiency of private property rights with respect to land and resource uses, and therefore an irrefutable justification for privatization.[1] This mistaken reading in part derives from Hardin's appeal to the metaphor of cattle, under the private ownership of several individuals concerned to maximize their individual utility, pastured on a piece of common land. The owners individually gain from adding cattle, while any losses in fertility from so doing are spread across all users. So all the herders continue to add cattle until the common land loses all productivity. If the cattle were held in common, of course, the metaphor would not work. This shows that it is private property in cattle and individual utility-maximizing behavior that lie at the heart of the problem, rather than the common-property character of the resource. But none of this was Hardin's fundamental concern. His preoccupation was population growth. The personal decision to have children would, he feared, eventually lead to the destruction of the global commons and the exhaustion of all resources (as Malthus also argued). The only solution, in his view, is authoritarian regulatory population control.[2]

I cite this example to highlight the way thinking about the commons has all too often itself become enclosed within far too narrow a set of presumptions, largely driven by the example of the land enclosures that occurred in Britain from the late medieval period onwards. As a result, thinking has often polarized between private property solutions and authoritarian state intervention. From a political perspective, the whole issue has been clouded over by a gut-reaction (laced with hefty doses of nostalgia for a once-upon-a-time supposedly moral economy of common action) either for or—more commonly on the left—against enclosure.

Elinor Ostrom seeks to disrupt some of the presumptions in her book, *Governing the Commons*.[3] She systematizes the anthropological, sociological, and historical evidence that had long shown that if the herders talked with each other (or had cultural rules of sharing) then they might easily solve any commons issue. Ostrom shows from innumerable examples that individuals can and often do devise ingenious and eminently sensible collective ways to manage common property resources for individual and collective benefit. Her concern was to establish why in some instances they succeed in so doing, and under what circumstances they might not. Her case studies "shatter the convictions of many policy analysts that the only way to solve CPR problems is for external authorities to impose full private property rights or centralized regulation." Instead, they demonstrate "rich mixtures of public and private instrumentalities." Armed with that conclusion, she could do battle with that economic orthodoxy that simply views policy in terms of a dichotomous choice between state and market.

But most of her examples involved as few as a hundred or so appropriators. Anything much larger (her largest example was 15,000 people), she found, required a "nested" structure of decision-making, because direct negotiation between all individuals was impossible. This implies that nested, and therefore in some sense "hierarchical" forms of organization are needed to address large-scale problems such as global warming. Unfortunately the term "hierarchy" is anathema in conventional thinking (Ostrom avoids it), and virulently unpopular with much of the left these days. The only politically correct form of organization in many radical circles is non-state, non-hierarchical, and horizontal. To avoid the implication that some sorts of nested hierarchical arrangements might be necessary, the question of how to manage the commons at large as opposed to small and local scales (for example, the global population problem that was Hardin's concern) tends to be evaded.

There is, clearly, an analytically difficult "scale problem" at work here that needs (but does not receive) careful evaluation. The possibilities for sensible management of common property resources that exist at one scale (such as shared water rights between one hundred farmers in a small river basin) do not and cannot carry over to problems such as global warming, or even to the regional diffusion of acid deposition from power stations. As we "jump scales" (as geographers like to put it), so the whole nature of the commons problem and the prospects of finding a solution change dramatically.[4] What looks like a good way to resolve problems at one scale does not hold at another scale. Even worse, patently good solutions at one scale (the "local," say) do not necessarily aggregate up (or cascade down) to make for good solutions at another scale (the global, for example). This is why Hardin's metaphor is so misleading: he uses a small-scale example of private capital operating on a common pasture to explicate a global problem, as if there is no problem whatsoever in shifting scales.

This is also, incidentally, why the valuable lessons gained from the collective organization of small-scale solidarity economies along common-property lines cannot translate into global solutions without resort to "nested" and therefore hierarchical organizational forms. Unfortunately, as already noted, the idea of hierarchy is anathema to many segments of the oppositional left these days. A fetishism of organizational preference (pure horizontality, for example) all too often stands in the way of exploring appropriate and effective solutions.[5] Just to be clear, I am not saying horizontality is bad—indeed, I think it an excellent objective—but that we should acknowledge its limits as a hegemonic organizational principle, and be prepared to go far beyond it when necessary.

There is much confusion also over the relationship between the commons and the supposed evils of enclosure. In the grander scheme of things (and particularly at the global level), some sort of enclosure is often the best way to preserve certain kinds of valued commons. That sounds like, and is, a contradictory statement, but it reflects a truly contradictory situation. It will take a draconian act of enclosure in Amazonia, for example, to protect both biodiversity *and* the cultures of indigenous populations as part of our global natural and cultural commons. It will almost certainly require state authority to protect those commons against the philistine democracy of short-term moneyed interests ravaging the land with soy bean plantations and cattle ranching. So not all forms of enclosure can be dismissed as bad by definition. The production and enclosure of non-commodified spaces in a ruthlessly commodifying world is surely a good thing. But in this instance there may be another problem: expelling indigenous populations from their forest lands (as the World Wide Fund for Nature often advocates) may be deemed necessary to preserve biodiversity. One common may be protected at the expense of another. When a nature reserve is fenced off, public access is denied. It is dangerous, however, to presume that the best way to preserve one sort of common is to deny another. There is plenty of evidence from joint forest management schemes, for example, that the dual objective of improving habitats and forest growth while maintaining access for traditional users to forest resources often ends up benefiting both. The idea of protecting the commons through enclosures is not always easily broached, however, when it needs to be actively explored as an anti-capitalist strategy. In fact a common demand on the left for "local autonomy" is actually a demand for some kind of enclosure.

Questions of the commons, we must conclude, are contradictory and therefore always contested. Behind these contestations lie conflicting social and political interests. Indeed, "politics," Jacques Rancière has remarked, "is the sphere of activity of a common that can only ever be contentious."[6] At the end of it all, the analyst is often left with a simple decision: Whose side are you on, whose common interests do you seek to protect, and by what means?

The rich these days have the habit, for example, of sealing themselves off in gated communities within which an exclusionary commons becomes defined. This is in principle no different than fifty users divvying up common water resources among themselves without regard for anyone else. The rich even have the gall to market their exclusionary urban spaces as a traditional village commons, as in the case of the Kierland Commons in Phoenix, Arizona, which is described as an "urban village with space for retail, restaurants, offices," and so on.[7] Radical groups can also procure spaces (sometimes through the exercise of private property rights, as when they collectively buy a building to be used for some progressive purpose) from which they can reach out to further a politics of common action. Or they can establish a commune or a soviet within some protected space. The politically active "houses of the people" that Margaret Kohn describes as central to political action in early twentieth century Italy were exactly of this sort.[8]

Not all forms of the common entail open access. Some (like the air we breathe) are, while others (like the streets of our cities) are in principle open, but regulated, policed, and even privately managed in the form of business improvement districts. Still others (like a common water resource controlled by fifty farmers) are from the very start exclusive to a particular social group. Most of Ostrom's examples in her first book were of the last sort. Furthermore, in her initial studies she limited her inquiry to so-called "natural" resources such as land, forests, water, fisheries, and the like. (I say "so-called" because all resources are technological, economic, and cultural appraisals, and therefore socially defined.)

Ostrom, along with many colleagues and collaborators, later went on to examine other forms of the commons, such as genetic materials, knowledge, cultural assets, and the like. These commons are also very much under assault these days through commodification and enclosure. Cultural commons become commodified (and often bowdlerized) by a heritage industry bent on Disneyfication, for example. Intellectual property and patenting rights over genetic materials and scientific knowledge more generally constitute one of the hottest topics of our times. When publishing companies charge for access to articles in the scientific and technical journals they publish, the problem of access to what should be common knowledge open to all is plain to see. Over the last twenty years or so there has been an explosion of studies and practical proposals, as well as fierce legal struggles over creating an open-access knowledge commons.[9]

Cultural and intellectual commons of this last sort are often not subject to the logic of scarcity, or to exclusionary uses of the sort that apply to most natural resources. We can all listen to the same radio broadcast or TV show at the same time without diminishing it. The cultural commons, Hardt and Negri write, "is dynamic, involving both the product of labor and the means of future production. This common is not only the earth we share but also the languages we create, the social practices we establish, the modes of sociality that define our relationships, and so forth." These commons are built up over time, and are in principle open to all.[10]

The human qualities of the city emerge out of our practices in the diverse spaces of the city even as those spaces are subject to enclosure, social control, and appropriation by both private and public/state interests. There is an important distinction here between public spaces and public goods, on the one hand, and the commons on the other. Public spaces and public goods in the city have always been a matter of state power and public administration, and such spaces and goods do not necessarily a commons make. Throughout the history of urbanization, the provision of public spaces and public goods (such as sanitation, public health, education, and the like) by either public or private means has been crucial for capitalist development.[11] To the degree that cities have been sites of vigorous class conflicts and struggles, so urban administrations have often been forced to supply public goods (such as affordable public housing, health care, education, paved streets, sanitation, and water) to an urbanized working class. While these public spaces and public goods contribute mightily to the qualities of the commons, it takes political action on the part of citizens and the people to appropriate them or to make them so. Public education becomes a common when social forces appropriate, protect, and enhance it for mutual benefit (three cheers for the PTA). Syntagma Square in Athens, Tahrir Square in Cairo, and the Plaza de Catalunya in Barcelona were public spaces that became an urban commons as people assembled there to express their political views and make demands. The street is a public space that has historically often been transformed by social action into the common of revolutionary movement, as well as into a site of bloody suppression.[12] There is always a struggle over how the production of and access to public space and public goods is to be regulated, by whom, and in whose interests. The struggle to appropriate the public spaces and public goods in the city for a common purpose is ongoing. But in order to protect the common it is often vital to protect the flow of public goods that underpin the qualities of the common. As neoliberal politics diminishes the financing of public goods, so it diminishes the available common, forcing social groups to find other ways to support that common (education, for example).

The common is not to be construed, therefore, as a particular kind of thing, asset or even social process, but as an unstable and malleable social relation between a particular self-defined social group and those aspects of its actually existing or yet-to-be-created social and/or physical environment deemed crucial to its life and livelihood. There is, in effect, a social practice of *commoning*. This practice produces or establishes a social relation with a common whose uses are either exclusive to a social group or partially or fully open to all and sundry. At the heart of the practice of commoning lies the principle that the relation between the social group and that aspect of the environment being treated as a common shall be both collective and non-commodified—off-limits to the logic of market exchange and market valuations. This last point is crucial because it helps distinguish between public goods construed as productive state expenditures and a common which is established or used in a completely different way and for a completely different purpose, even when it ends up indirectly enhancing the wealth and income of the social group that claims it. A community garden can thus be viewed as a good thing in itself, no matter what food may be produced there. This does not prevent some of the food being sold.

Plainly, many different social groups can engage in the practice of commoning for many different reasons. This takes us back to the foundational question of which social groups should be supported and which should not in the course of commoning struggles. The ultra-rich, after all, are just as fiercely protective of their residential commons as anyone, and have far more fire-power and influence in creating and protecting them.

The common, even—and particularly—when it cannot be enclosed, can always be traded upon even though it is not in itself a commodity. The ambience and attractiveness of a city, for example, is a collective product of its citizens, but it is the tourist trade that commercially capitalizes upon that common to extract monopoly rents (see Chapter 4). Through their daily activities and struggles, individuals and social groups create the social world of the city, and thereby create something common as a framework within which all can dwell. While this culturally creative common cannot be destroyed through use, it can be degraded and banalized through excessive abuse. Streets that get clogged with traffic make that particular public space almost unusable even for drivers (let alone pedestrians and protestors), leading at some point to the levying of congestion and access charges in an attempt to restrict use so that it can function more efficiently. This kind of street is not a common. Before the car came along, however, streets were often a common—a place of popular sociality, a play space for kids (I am old enough to remember that was where we played all the time). But that kind of common was destroyed and turned into a public space dominated by the advent of the automobile (prompting attempts by city administrations to recover some aspects of a "more civilized" common past by organizing pedestrian precincts, sidewalk cafés, bike paths, pocket parks as play spaces, and the like). But such attempts to create new kinds of urban commons can all too easily be capitalized upon. In fact they may be designed precisely with that in mind. Urban parks almost always increase nearby residential property prices in surrounding areas (provided, of course, that the public space of the park is regulated and patrolled to keep the riff-raff and the drug dealers out). The newly created High Line in New York City has had a tremendous impact on nearby residential property values, thus denying access to affordable housing in the area for most of the citizens of New York City by virtue of rapidly rising rents. The creation of this kind of public space radically diminishes rather than enhances the potentiality of commoning for all but the very rich.

The real problem here, as in Hardin's original morality tale, is not the commons per se, but the failure of individualized private property rights to fulfill common interests in the way they are supposed to do. Why do we not, therefore, focus on the individual ownership of the cattle and individual utility-maximizing behavior, rather than the common pasture, as the basic problem to be addressed? The justification for private property rights in liberal theory, after all, is that they should serve to maximize the common good when socially integrated through the institutions of fair and free market exchange. A commonwealth (said Hobbes) is produced through privatizing competitive interests within a framework of strong state power. This opinion, articulated by liberal theorists such as John Locke and Adam Smith, continues to be preached. These days, the trick, of course, is to downplay the need for strong state power while in fact deploying it—sometimes brutally. The solution to the problems of global poverty, the World Bank continues to assure us (leaning heavily on the theories of de Soto), is private property rights for all slum-dwellers and access to micro-finance (which just happens to yield the world's financiers hefty rates of return while driving not a few participants to commit suicide in the face of debt peonage).[13] Yet the myth prevails: once the inherent entrepreneurial instincts of the poor are liberated as a force of nature, it is said, then all will be well and the problem of chronic poverty will be broken and the common wealth enhanced. This was indeed the argument made in support of the original enclosure movement in Britain from the late medieval period on. And it was not entirely wrong.

For Locke, individual property is a natural right that arises when individuals create value by mixing their labor with the land. The fruits of their labor belong to them and to them alone. This was the essence of Locke's version of the labor theory of value.[14] Market exchange socializes that right when each individual gets back the value they have created by exchanging it against an equivalent value created by another. In effect, individuals maintain, extend, and socialize their private property right through value-creation and supposedly free and fair market exchange. This is how, says Adam Smith, the wealth of nations is most easily created and the common good best served. He was not entirely wrong.

The presumption is, however, that markets can be fair and free, and in classical political economy it was assumed that the state would intervene to make them so (at least that is what Adam Smith advises statesmen to do). But there is an ugly corollary to Locke's theory. Individuals who fail to produce value have no claim to property. The dispossession of indigenous populations in North America by "productive" colonists was justified because indigenous populations did not produce value.[15]

So how does Marx deal with all of this? Marx accepts the Lockean fiction in the opening chapters of *Capital* (though the argument is certainly larded with irony when, for example, he takes up the strange role of the Robinson Crusoe myth in political-economic thinking, in which someone thrown into a state of nature acts like a true-born entrepreneurial Briton).[16] But when Marx takes up how labor-power becomes an individualized commodity that is bought and sold in fair and free markets, we see the Lockean fiction unmasked for what it really is: a system founded on equality in value-exchange produces surplus value for the capitalist owner of the means of production through the exploitation of living labor in production (not in the market, where bourgeois rights and constitutionalities can prevail).

The Lockean formulation is even more dramatically undermined when Marx takes up the question of collective labor. In a world where individual artisan producers controlling their own means of production could engage in free exchange in relatively free markets, the Lockean fiction might have some purchase. But the rise of the factory system from the late eighteenth century onwards, Marx argued, rendered Locke's theoretical formulations redundant (even if they had not been redundant in the first place). In the factory, labor is collectively organized. If there is any property right to be derived from this form of laboring, it would surely have to be a collective or associated rather than individual property right. The definition of value-producing labor, which grounds Locke's theory of private property, no longer holds for the individual, but is shifted to the collective laborer. Communism should then arise on the basis of "an association of free men, working with the means of production held in common, and expending their many different forms of labour-power in full self-awareness as one single labour force."[17] Marx does not advocate state ownership, but some form of ownership vested in the collective laborer producing for the common good.

How that form of ownership might come into being is established by turning Locke's argument on the production of value against itself. Suppose, says Marx, that a capitalist begins production with a capital of $1,000 and in the first year manages to gain $200 surplus value from laborers mixing their labor with the land, and then uses that surplus in personal consumption. Then, after five years, the $1,000 should belong to the collective laborers, since they are the ones who have mixed their labor with the land. The capitalist has consumed away all his or her original wealth.[18] Like the indigenous populations of North America, capitalists deserve to lose their rights, according to this logic, since they themselves have produced no value.

While this idea sounds outrageous, it lay behind the Swedish Meidner plan proposed in the late 1960s.[19] The receipts from a tax placed on corporate profits, in return for wage restraint on the part of unions, were to be placed in a worker-controlled fund that would invest in and eventually buy out the corporation, thus bringing it under the common control of the associated laborers. Capital resisted this idea with all its might, and it was never implemented. But the idea ought to be reconsidered. The central conclusion is that the collective laboring that is now productive of value must ground collective not individual property rights. Value—socially necessary labor time—is the capitalist common, and it is represented by money, the universal equivalent in which common wealth is measured. The common is not, therefore, something that existed once upon a time that has since been lost, but something that is, like the urban commons, continuously being produced. The problem is that it is just as continuously being enclosed and appropriated by capital in its commodified and monetized form, even as it is being continuously produced by collective labor.

The primary means by which it is appropriated in urban contexts is, of course, through the extraction of land and property rents.[20] A community group that struggles to maintain ethnic diversity in its neighborhood and protect against gentrification may suddenly find its property prices (and taxes) rising as real estate agents market the "character" of their neighborhood to the wealthy as multicultural, street-lively, and diverse. By the time the market has done its destructive work, not only have the original residents been dispossessed of that common which they had created (often being forced out by rising rents and property taxes), but the common itself becomes so debased as to be unrecognizable. Neighborhood revitalization through gentrification in South Baltimore displaced a lively street life, where people sat on their stoops on warm summer nights and conversed with neighbors, with air-conditioned and burglar-proofed houses with a BMW parked out front and a rooftop deck, but with no one to be seen on the street. Revitalization meant devitalization, according to local opinion. This is the fate that again and again threatens places like Christiania in Copenhagen, the St. Pauli districts of Hamburg, or Willamsburg and DUMBO in New York City, and it was also what destroyed that city's SoHo district.

This is, surely, a far better tale by which to explicate the true tragedy of the urban commons for our times. Those who create an interesting and stimulating everyday neighborhood life lose it to the predatory practices of the real estate entrepreneurs, the financiers and upper class consumers bereft of any urban social imagination. The better the common qualities a social group creates, the more likely it is to be raided and appropriated by private profit-maximizing interests.

But there is a further analytic point here that must be remarked. The collective labor that Marx envisaged was for the most part confined to the factory. What if we broaden that conception to think, as Hardt and Negri suggest, that it is the metropolis that now constitutes a vast common produced by the collective labor expended on and in the city? The right to use that common must surely then be accorded to all those who have had a part in producing it. This is, of course, the basis for the claim to the right to the city on the part of the collective laborers who have made it. The struggle for the right to the city is against the powers of capital that ruthlessly feed upon and extract rents from the common life that others have produced. This reminds us that the real problem lies with the private character of property rights and the power these rights confer to appropriate not only the labor but also the collective products of others. Put another way, the problem is not the common per se, but the relations between those who produce or capture it at a variety of scales and those who appropriate it for private gain. Much of the corruption that attaches to urban politics relates to how public investments are allocated to produce something that looks like a common but which promotes gains in private asset values for privileged property owners. The distinction between urban public goods and urban commons is both fluid and dangerously porous. How often are developmental projects subsidized by the state in the name of the common interest when the true beneficiaries are a few landholders, financiers, and developers?

How, then, are urban commons produced, organized, used, and appropriated across a whole metropolitan area? How commoning might work at the local neighborhood level is relatively clear. It involves some mix of individual and private initiative to organize and capture externality effects while putting some aspect of the environment outside of the market. The local state is involved through regulations, codes, standards, and public investments, along with informal and formal neighborhood organization (for example, a community association which may or may not be politically active and militant, depending on the circumstances). There are many cases in which territorial strategies and enclosures within the urban milieu can become a vehicle for the political left to advance its cause. The organizers of low-income and precarious labor in Baltimore declared the whole Inner Harbor area a "human rights zone"—a sort of common—where every worker should receive a living wage. The place-bound Federation of Neighborhood Associations in El Alto became one of the key bases of the El Alto rebellions of 2003 and 2005, in which the whole city became collectively mobilized against the dominant forms of political power.[21] Enclosure is a temporary political means to pursue a common political end.

The general outcome that Marx describes still holds, however: capital, impelled onwards by the coercive laws of competition to maximize utility (profitability)—as do the cattle owners in Hardin's tale—produces

> progress in the art, not only of robbing the worker, but of robbing the
> soil; all progress in increasing the fertility of the soil for a given time is a

progress towards ruining the more long-lasting sources of that fertility. The more a country proceeds from large-scale industry as the background of its development, as in the case of the United States, the more rapid is this process of destruction. Capitalist production, therefore, only develops the techniques and the degree of combination of the social process of production by simultaneously undermining the original sources of all wealth—the soil and the worker.[22]

Capitalist urbanization perpetually tends to destroy the city as a social, political and livable commons.

This "tragedy" is similar to that which Hardin depicts, but the logic from which it arises is entirely different. Left unregulated, individualized capital accumulation perpetually threatens to destroy the two basic common property resources that undergird all forms of production: the laborer and the land. But the land we now inhabit is a product of collective human labor. Urbanization is about the perpetual production of an urban commons (or its shadow-form of public spaces and public goods) and its perpetual appropriation and destruction by private interests. And with capital accumulation occurring at a compound rate of growth (usually at the minimum satisfactory level of 3 percent), so these dual threats to the environment (both "natural" and built) and to labor escalate in scale and intensity over time.[23] Look at the urban wreckage in Detroit to get a sense of how devastating this process can be.

But what is so interesting about the concept of the urban commons is that it poses all of the political contradictions of the commons in highly concentrated form. Consider, for example, the question of scale within which we move from the question of local neighborhoods and political organization to the metropolitan region as a whole. Traditionally, questions of the commons at the metropolitan level have been handled through mechanisms of state regional and urban planning, in recognition of the fact that the common resources required for urban populations to function effectively, such as water provision, transportation, sewage disposal, and open space for recreation, have to be provided at a metropolitan, regional scale. But when it comes to bundling together issues of this kind, left-analysis typically becomes vague, gesturing hopefully towards some magical concordance of local actions that will be effective at a regional or global level, or simply noting this as an important problem before moving back to that scale—usually the micro and the local—at which they feel most comfortable.

We can here learn something of the recent history of commons thinking in more conventional circles. Ostrom, for example, while dwelling in her Nobel Prize lecture on small-scale cases, takes refuge in her subtitle of "Polycentric Governance of Complex Economic Systems" to suggest she has some solution to commons issues across a variety of scales. In fact, all she does is gesture hopefully to the idea that "when a common-pool resource is closely connected to a larger social-ecological system, governance activities are organized in multiple nested layers," but without resort, she insists, to any monocentric hierarchical structure.[24]

The crucial problem here is to figure out how a polycentric governance system (or something analogous, such as Murray Bookchin's confederation of libertarian municipalities) might actually work, and to make sure that it does not mask something very different. This question is one that bedevils not only Ostrom's arguments, but a very wide range of radical left communalist proposals to address the problem of the commons. For this reason, it is very important to get the critique right.

In a paper prepared for a conference on Global Climate Change, Ostrom elaborated further on the nature of the argument which rests, conveniently for us, on results from a long-term study of the delivery of public goods in municipal regions.[25] The assumption had long been that the consolidation of public service provision into large-scale metropolitan forms of government, as opposed to their organization into numerous seemingly chaotic local administrations, would improve efficiency and effectiveness. But the studies convincingly showed this not to be so. The reasons all boiled down to how much easier it was to organize and enforce collective and cooperative action with strong participation of local inhabitants in smaller jurisdictions, and to the fact that the capacity for participation diminished rapidly with larger sizes of administrative unit. Ostrom ends by citing Andrew Sancton to the effect that

> municipalities are more than just providers of services. They are democratic mechanisms through which territorially based communities of people govern themselves at a local level … those who would force municipalities to amalgamate with each other invariably claim that their motive is to make municipalities stronger. Such an approach—however well-

intentioned—erodes the foundations of our liberal democracies because it undermines the notion that there can be forms of self-government that exist outside the institutions of the central government.[26]

Beyond market efficiency and effectiveness, there is a non-commodifiable reason to go to a smaller scale.

"While large-scale units were part of effective governance of metro-politan regions," Ostrom concludes, "small and medium-scale units were also necessary components." The constructive role of these smaller units, she argued, "needs to be seriously rethought." The question then arises of how relations between the smaller units might be structured. The answer, says Vincent Ostrom, is as a "polycentric order" in which "many elements are capable of making mutual adjustments ordering their relationships with one another within a general system of rules where each element acts with independence of other elements."[27]

So what is wrong with this picture? This whole argument has its roots in the so-called "Tiebout hypothesis." What Tiebout proposed was a fragmented metropolis in which many jurisdictions would each offer a particular local tax regime and a particular bundle of public goods to prospective residents, who would "vote with their feet" and chose that particular mix of taxes and services that suited their own needs and pref-erences.[28] At first glance the proposal seems very attractive. The problem is that the richer you are the more easily you can vote with your feet and pay the entry price of property and land costs. Superior public edu-cation may be provided at the cost of high property prices and taxes, but the poor are deprived of access to the superior public education and are condemned to live in a poor jurisdiction with poor public educa-tion. The resultant reproduction of class privilege and power through polycentric governance fits neatly into neoliberal class strategies of social reproduction.

Along with many more radical proposals for decentralized autonomy, Ostrom's is in danger of falling into exactly this trap. Neoliberal politics actually favors both administrative decentralization and the maximiza-tion of local autonomy. While on the one hand this opens a space within which radical forces can more easily plant the seeds of a more revolu-tionary agenda, the counter-revolutionary takeover of Cochabamba in the name of autonomy by the forces of reaction in 2007 (until they were forced out by popular rebellion) suggests that the embrace of localism and autonomy by much of the left as a pure strategy is problematic. In the United States, the leadership of the Cleveland initiative celebrated as an example of autonomous communitarianism in action supported the election of a radically right-wing and anti-union republican for governor.

Decentralization and autonomy are primary vehicles for producing greater inequality through neoliberalization. Thus, in New York State, the unequal provision of public education services across jurisdictions with radically different financial resources has been deemed by the courts as unconstitutional, and the state is under court order to move towards greater equalization of educational provision. It has failed to do so, and now uses the fiscal emergency as a further excuse to delay action. But note well, it is the higher-order and hierarchically determined mandate of the state courts that is crucial in mandating greater equality of treatment as a constitutional right. Ostrom does not rule out such higher-order rule-making. Relations between independent and autonomously functioning communities have to be established and regulated somehow (hence Vincent Ostrom's reference to "established rules"). But we are left in the dark as to how such higher-order rules might be constituted, by whom, and how they might be open to democratic control. For the whole metropolitan region some such rules (or customary practices) are both necessary and crucial. Furthermore, such rules must not only be established and asserted. They must also be enforced and actively policed (as is the case with any common). We need look no further than the "polycentric" Eurozone for a catastrophic example of what can go wrong: all members were supposed to abide by rules restricting their budgetary deficits, and when most of them broke the rules there was no way to force compliance or deal with the fiscal imbalances that then emerged between states. Getting states to comply with carbon emissions targets appears an equally hopeless task. While the historical answer to the question "Who puts the 'common' into the Common Market?" may correctly be depicted as embodying everything that is wrong about hierarchical forms of governance, the alternative imaginary of thousands upon thousands of autonomous municipalities fiercely defending their autonomy and their turf while endlessly (and undoubtedly acrimoniously) negotiating their position within Europe-wide divisions of labor is hardly alluring. ✁

How can radical decentralization—surely a worthwhile objective—work without constituting some higher-order hierarchical authority? It is simply naïve to believe that polycentrism or any other form of decentralization can work without strong hierarchical constraints and active enforcement. Much of the radical left—particularly of an anarchist and autonomist persuasion—has no answer to this problem. State interventions (to say nothing of state enforcement and policing) are unacceptable, and the legitimacy of bourgeois constitutionality is generally denied. Instead there is the vague and naïve hope that social groups who have organized their relations to their local commons satisfactorily will do the right thing or converge upon some satisfactory inter-group practices through negotiation and interaction. For this to occur, local groups would have to be untroubled by any externality effects that their actions might have on the rest of the world, and to give up accrued advantages, democratically distributed within the social group, in order to rescue or supplement the well-being of near (let alone distant) others, who as a result of either bad decisions or misfortune have fallen into a state of starvation and misery. History provides us with very little evidence that such redistributions can work on anything other than an occasional or one-off basis. There is, therefore, nothing whatsoever to prevent escalating social inequalities between communities. This accords all too well with the neoliberal project of not only protecting but further privileging structures of class power (of the sort so clearly evident in the New York State school financing debacle).

Murray Bookchin is acutely aware of such dangers—the "agenda of a libertarian municipalism can easily become vacuous at best or be used for highly parochial ends at worst," he writes. His answer is "confederalism." While municipal assemblies working through direct democracy form the policy-making base, the state is replaced "by a confederal network of municipal assemblies; the corporate economy reduced to a truly political economy in which municipalities, interacting with each other economically as well as politically, will resolve their material problems as citizen bodies in open assemblies." These confederal assemblies will be given over to administration and governance of policies determined in the municipal assemblies, and the delegates will be recallable and answerable at all times to the will of the municipal assemblies. The confederal councils

> become the means for interlinking villages, towns, neighborhoods, and cities into confederal networks. Power thus flows from the bottom up instead of from the top down, and in confederations, the flow of power from the bottom up diminishes with the scope of the federal council ranging territorially from localities and regions and from regions to ever-broader territorial areas.[29]

Bookchin's proposal is by far the most sophisticated radical proposal to deal with the creation and collective use of the commons across a variety of scales, and is well worth elaborating as part of the radical anti-capitalist agenda.

This issue is all the more pressing because of the violent neoliberal attack upon the public provision of social public goods over the last thirty years or more. This corresponded to the root-and-branch attack upon the rights and power of organized labor that began in the 1970s (from Chile to Britain), but it focused on the costs of social reproduction of labor directly. Capital has long preferred to treat the costs of social reproduction as an externality—a cost for which it bears no market responsibility—but the social-democratic movement and the active threat of a communist alternative forced capital to internalize some of those costs, along with some of the externality costs attributable to environmental degradation, up until the 1970s in the advanced capitalist world. The aim of neoliberal policies since 1980 or so has been to dump these costs into the global commons of social reproduction and the environment, creating, as it were, a negative commons in which whole populations are forced now to dwell. Questions of social reproduction, gender, and the commons are interlinked.[30]

The response on the part of capital to the global crisis conditions after 2007 has been to implement a draconian global austerity plan that diminishes the supply of public goods to support both social reproduction and environmental amelioration, thereby diminishing the qualities of the commons in both instances. It has also used the crisis to facilitate even more predatory activity in the private appropriation of the commons as a necessary precondition for the revival of growth. The uses of eminent domain, for example, to appropriate spaces for private purposes (as opposed to the "public utility" for which such laws were originally intended) is a classic case of the redefinition of public purpose as state-led sponsorship of private development.

From California to Greece, the crisis produced losses in urban asset values, rights, and entitlements for the mass of the population, coupled with the extension of predatory capitalist power over low-income and hitherto marginalized populations. It was, in short, a wholesale attack upon the reproductive and environmental commons. Living on less than $2 a day, a global population of more than 2 billion or so is now being taken in by microfinance as the "subprime of all subprime forms of lending," so as to extract wealth from them (as happened in US housing markets through sub-prime predatory lending followed by foreclosures) to gild the MacMansions of the rich. The environmental commons are no less threatened, while the proposed answers (such as carbon trading and new environmental technologies) merely propose that we seek to exit the impasse using the same tools of capital accumulation and speculative market exchange that got us into the difficulties in the first place. It is unsurprising, therefore, not only that the poor are still with us, but that their numbers grow rather than diminish over time. While India has been racking up a respectable record of growth throughout this crisis, for example, the number of billionaires has leapt from 26 to 69 in the last three years, while the number of slum-dwellers has nearly doubled over the last decade. The urban impacts are quite stunning, as luxurious air-conditioned condominiums arise in the midst of uncared-for urban squalor, out of which impoverished people struggle mightily to make some sort of acceptable existence for themselves.

The dismantling of the regulatory frameworks and controls that sought, however inadequately, to curb the penchant for predatory practices of accumulation has unleashed the *après moi le déluge* logic of unbridled accumulation and financial speculation that has now turned into a veritable flood of creative destruction, including that wrought through capitalist urbanization. This damage can only be contained and reversed by the socialization of surplus production and distribution, and the establishment of a new common of wealth open to all.

It is in this context that the revival of a rhetoric and theory of the commons takes on an added significance. If state-supplied public goods either decline or become a mere vehicle for private accumulation (as is happening to education), and if the state withdraws from their provision, then there is only one possible response, which is for populations to self-organize to provide their own commons (as happened in Bolivia, as we shall see in Chapter 5). The political recognition that the commons can be produced, protected, and used for social benefit becomes a framework for resisting capitalist power and rethinking the politics of an anti-capitalist transition.

But what matters here is not the particular mix of institutional arrangements—the enclosures here, the extensions of a variety of collective and common-property arrangements there—but that the unified effect of political action address the spiraling degradation of labor and land resources (including the resources embedded in the "second nature" of the built environment) at the hands of capital. In this effort, the "rich mix of instrumentalities" that Elinor Ostrom begins to identify—not only public and private, but collective and associational, nested, hierarchical and horizontal, exclusionary and open—will all have a key role to play in finding ways to organize production, distribution, exchange, and consumption in order to meet human wants and needs on an anti-capitalist basis. This rich mix is not given, but has to be constructed.

The point is not to fulfill the requirements of accumulation for accumulation's sake on the part of the class that appropriates the common wealth from the class that produces it. The return of the commons as a political question has to be integrated wholly into anti-capitalist struggle in a very specific way. Unfortunately the idea of the commons (like the right to the city) is just as easily appropriated by existing political power as is the value to be extracted from an actual urban common by real estate interests. The point, therefore, is to change all that and to find creative ways to use the powers of collective labor for the common good, and to keep the value produced under the control of the laborers who produced it.

This requires a double-pronged political attack, through which the state is forced to supply more and more in the way of public goods for public purposes, along with the self-organization of whole populations to appropriate, use, and supplement those goods in ways that extend and enhance the qualities of the non-commodified reproductive and environmental commons. The production, protection, and use of public goods and the urban commons in cities like Mumbai, São Paulo, Johannesburg, Los Angeles, Shanghai, and Tokyo becomes a central issue for democratic social movements to address. And that will take much more imagination and sophistication than is currently brought to bear in the hegemonic radical theories of the commons currently circulating, particularly as these commons are being continuously created and appropriated through the capitalist form of urbanization. The role of the commons in city formation and in urban politics is only now being clearly acknowledged and worked upon, both theoretically and in the world of radical practice. There is much work to do, but there are abundant signs in the urban social movements occurring around the world that there are plenty of people and a critical mass of political energy available to do it.

CHAPTER FOUR

The Art of Rent

The number of workers engaged in cultural activities and production has increased considerably over the past few decades (from some 150,000 artists registered in the New York metropolitan region in the early 1980s to likely more than double that by now), and continues to rise. They form the creative core of what Daniel Bell calls "the cultural mass" (not the creators but the transmitters of culture in the media and elsewhere),[1] and have shifted in their political stances over the years. In the 1960s, the art colleges were hotbeds of radical discussion, but their subsequent pacification and professionalization has seriously diminished agitational politics. Though socialist strategy and thought may need to be reconfigured, revitalizing such institutions as centers of political engagement and mobilizing the political and agitational powers of cultural producers is surely a worthwhile objective for the left. While commercialization and market incentives unquestionably dominate in these times, there are plenty of dissident sub-currents and discontents to be detected among cultural producers to make this a fertile field for critical expression and political agitation for the production of a new kind of commons.

That culture is a form of commons, and that it has become a commodity of some sort, is undeniable. Yet there is also a widespread belief that there is something so special about certain cultural products and events (be they in the arts, theater, music, cinema, architecture, or more broadly in localized ways of life, heritage, collective memories, and affective communities) as to set them apart from ordinary commodities like shirts and shoes. While the boundary between the two sorts of commodities is highly porous (perhaps increasingly so), there are still grounds for maintaining an analytic separation. It may be, of course, that we distinguish cultural artifacts and events because we cannot bear to think of them as anything other than authentically different, existing on some higher plane of human creativity and meaning than that located in the factories of mass production and consumption. But even when we strip away all residues of wishful thinking (often backed by powerful ideologies), we are still left with something very special about those products designated as "cultural." Art studio and gallery districts, and strips of cafés and bars where musicians meet and play, are not the same as clothing stores simply because they too can only exist if they turn enough profit to pay their rent. How, then, can the commodity status of so many of these phenomena be reconciled with their special character?

MONOPOLY RENT AND COMPETITION

To the cultural producers themselves, usually more interested in affairs of aesthetics (sometimes even dedicated to ideals of art for art's sake), of affective values, of social life and of the heart, a term like "monopoly rent" might appear far too technical and arid to bear much weight beyond the possible calculi of the financier, the developer, the real estate speculator, and the landlord. But I hope to show that it has a much grander purchase: that, properly constructed, it can generate rich interpretations of the many practical and personal dilemmas arising in the nexus between capitalist globalization, local political-economic developments, and the evolution of cultural meanings and aesthetic values.[2]

All rent is based on the monopoly power of private owners over certain assets. Monopoly rent arises because social actors can realize an enhanced income stream over an extended time by virtue of their exclusive control over some directly or indirectly tradable item which is in some crucial respects unique and non-replicable. There are two situations in which the category of monopoly rent comes to the fore. The first arises because social actors control some special quality resource, commodity, or location which, in relation to a certain kind of activity, enables them to extract monopoly rents from those desiring to use it. In the realm of production, Marx argues, the most obvious example is the vineyard producing wine of extraordinary quality that can be sold at a monopoly price. In this circumstance "the monopoly price creates the rent."[3] The locational version would be centrality (for the commercial capitalist) relative to, say, the transport and communications network, or proximity (for the hotel chain) to some highly concentrated activity (such as a financial center). The commercial capitalist and the hotelier are willing to pay a premium for the land because of its accessibility.

These are the indirect cases of monopoly rent. It is not the land, resource or location of unique qualities which is traded, but the commodity or service produced through their use. In the second case, the land, resource or asset is directly traded upon (as when vineyards or prime real estate sites are sold to multinational capitalists and financiers for speculative purposes). Scarcity can be created by withholding the land, resource, or asset from current uses and speculating on future values. Monopoly rent of this sort can be extended to ownership of works of art, such as a Rodin or a Picasso, which can be (and increasingly are) bought and sold as investments. It is the uniqueness of the Picasso or the site which here forms the basis for the monopoly price.

The two forms of monopoly rent often intersect. A vineyard (with its unique château and beautiful physical setting) renowned for its wines can be traded at a monopoly price directly, as can the uniquely flavored wines produced on its land. A Picasso can be purchased for capital gain and then leased to someone else who puts it on view for a monopoly price. The proximity to a financial center can be traded directly as well as indirectly to, say, the hotel chain that uses it for its own purposes. But the difference between the two rental forms is important. It is unlikely (though not impossible), for example, that Westminster Abbey and Buckingham Palace will be traded directly (even the most ardent privatizers might balk at that). But they can be and plainly are traded *upon* through the marketing practices of the tourist industry (or, in the case of Buckingham Palace, by the Queen).

Two contradictions attach to the category of monopoly rent. Both of

them are important to the argument that follows. First, while uniqueness and particularity are crucial to the definition of "special qualities,"
the requirement of tradability means that no item can be so unique or
so special as to be entirely outside the monetary calculus. The Picasso
has to have a money value, as does the Monet, the Manet, the aborigi-
nal art, the archaeological artifacts, the historic buildings, the ancient
monuments, the Buddhist temples, and the experience of rafting down
the Colorado, or of being in Istanbul or on top of Everest. There is, as is
evident from such a list, a certain difficulty of "market formation" here.
For while markets have formed around works of art, and to some degree
around archaeological artifacts, there are plainly several items on this list
that are hard to incorporate directly into a market (this is the problem
with Westminster Abbey). Many items may not even be easy to trade
upon indirectly.

The contradiction here is that the more easily marketable such items
become, the less unique and special they appear. In some instances the
marketing itself tends to destroy the unique qualities (particularly if
these depend on qualities such as wilderness, remoteness, the purity of
some aesthetic experience, and the like). More generally, to the degree
that such items or events are easily marketable (and subject to replica-
tion by forgeries, fakes, imitations, or simulacra), the less they provide a
basis for monopoly rent. I am put in mind here of the student who com-
plained about how inferior her experience of Europe was compared to
Disney World:

> At Disney World all the countries are much closer together, and they show
> you the best of each country. Europe is boring. People talk strange lan-
> guages and things are dirty. Sometimes you don't see anything interesting
> in Europe for days, but at Disney World something different happens all
> the time and people are happy. It's much more fun. It's well designed.[4]

While this sounds a laughable judgment, it is sobering to reflect on how
much Europe is attempting to redesign itself to Disney standards (and
not only for the benefit of American tourists). But—and here is the heart
of the contradiction—the more Europe becomes Disneyfied, the less
unique and special it is. The bland homogeneity that goes with pure commodification erases monopoly advantages; cultural products become no

different from commodities in general. "The advanced transformation of consumer goods into corporate products or 'trade mark articles' that hold a monopoly on aesthetic value," writes Wolfgang Haug, "has by and large replaced the elementary or 'generic' products," so that "commodity aesthetics" extends its border "further and further into the realm of cultural industries."[5] Conversely, every capitalist seeks to persuade consumers of the unique and non-replicable qualities of their commodities (hence name brands, advertising, and the like). Pressures from both sides threaten to squeeze out the unique qualities that underlie monopoly rents. If the latter are to be sustained and realized, therefore, some way has to be found to keep some commodities or places unique and particular *enough* (and I will later reflect on what this might mean) to maintain a monopolistic edge in an otherwise commodified and often fiercely competitive economy.

But why, in a neoliberal world where competitive markets are supposedly dominant, would monopoly of any sort be tolerated, let alone seen as desirable? We here encounter the second contradiction which, at root, turns out to be a mirror image of the first. Competition, as Marx long ago observed, always tends towards monopoly (or oligopoly) simply because the survival of the fittest in the war of all against all eliminates the weaker firms.[6] The fiercer the competition, the faster the trend towards oligopoly, if not monopoly. It is therefore no accident that the liberalization of markets and the celebration of market competition in recent years have produced incredible centralization of capital (Microsoft, Rupert Murdoch, Bertelsmann, financial services, and a wave of takeovers, mergers and consolidations in airlines, retailing and even in older industries like automobiles, petroleum, and the like). This tendency has long been recognized as a troublesome feature of capitalist dynamics—hence the antitrust legislation in the United States and the work of the Monopolies and Mergers Commissions in Europe. But these are weak defenses against an overwhelming force.

This structural dynamic would not have the importance it does were it not for the fact that capitalists actively cultivate monopoly powers. They thereby realize far-reaching control over production and marketing, and hence stabilize their business environment to allow for rational calculation and long-term planning, the reduction of risk and uncertainty, and more generally guarantee themselves a relatively peaceful and untroubled existence. The visible hand of the corporation, as Alfred Chandler terms it, has consequently been of far greater importance to capitalist historical geography than the invisible hand of the market made so much of by Adam Smith, and paraded ad nauseam before us in recent years as the guiding power in the neoliberal ideology of contemporary globalization.[7]

But it is here that the mirror image of the first contradiction comes most clearly into view: market processes crucially depend upon the individual monopoly of capitalists (of all sorts) over ownership of the means of production, including finance and land. All rent, recall, is a return to the monopoly power of private ownership of some crucial asset, such as land or a patent. The monopoly power of private property is therefore both the beginning-point and the end-point of all capitalist activity. A non-tradable juridical right exists at the very foundation of all capitalist trade, making the option of non-trading (hoarding, withholding, miserly behavior) an important problem in capitalist markets. Pure market competition, free commodity exchange, and perfect market rationality are therefore rather rare and chronically unstable devices for coordinating production and consumption decisions. The problem is to keep economic relations competitive *enough* while sustaining the individual and class monopoly privileges of private property that are the foundation of capitalism as a political-economic system.

This last point demands one further elaboration to bring us closer to the topic at hand. It is widely but erroneously assumed that monopoly power of the grand and culminating sort is most clearly signaled by the centralization and concentration of capital in mega-corporations. Conversely, small firm size is widely assumed, again erroneously, to be a sign of a competitive market situation. By this measure, a once-competitive capitalism has become increasingly monopolized over time. This error arises in part because of a rather too facile application of Marx's arguments concerning the "law of the tendency for the centralization of capital," which ignores his counter-argument that centralization "would soon bring about the collapse of capitalist production if it were not for counteracting tendencies, which have a continuous decentralizing effect."[8] But it is also supported by an economic theory of the firm that generally ignores its spatial and locational context, even though it does accept (on those rare occasions where it deigns to consider the matter) that locational advantage involves "monopolistic competition."

In the nineteenth century, for example, the brewer, the baker, and the candlestick maker were all protected to considerable degree from competition in local markets by the high cost of transportation. Local monopoly powers were omnipresent (even though firms were small in size), and very hard to break, in everything from energy to food supply. By this measure, small-scale nineteenth-century capitalism was far less competitive than now. It is at this point that the changing conditions of transport and communications enter in as crucial determining variables. As spatial barriers diminished through the capitalist penchant for "the annihilation of space through time," many local industries and services lost their local protections and monopoly privileges.[9] They were forced into competition with producers in other locations—at first relatively nearby, but then much farther away.

The historical geography of the brewing trade is very instructive in this regard. In the nineteenth century most people drank local brew because they had no choice. By the end of the nineteenth century beer produc-tion and consumption in Britain had been regionalized to a considerable degree, and remained so until the 1960s (foreign imports, with the excep-tion of Guinness, were unheard of). But then the market became national (Newcastle Brown and Scottish Youngers appeared in London and the South), before becoming international (imports suddenly became all the rage). If one drinks local brew now it is by choice, usually out of some mix of principled attachment to locality and some special quality of the beer (based on the technique, the water, or whatever) that differentiates it from others. There are bars in Manhattan where you can drink different local brews from all over the world!

Plainly, the economic space of competition has changed in both form and scale over time. The recent bout of globalization has signifi-cantly diminished the monopoly protections given historically by high transport and communications costs, while the removal of institutional barriers to trade (protectionism) has likewise diminished the monopoly rents to be procured by keeping foreign competition out. But capital-ism cannot do without monopoly powers, and craves means to assemble them. So the question upon the agenda is how to assemble monopoly powers in a situation where the protections afforded by the so-called "natural monopolies" of space and location, and the political protections of national boundaries and tariffs, have been seriously diminished, if not eliminated.

The obvious answer is to centralize capital in mega-corporations or set up looser alliances (as in the airline and automobile industries) that dominate markets. And we have seen plenty of that. The second path is to secure ever more firmly the monopoly rights of private property through international commercial laws that regulate all global trade. Patents and so-called "intellectual property rights" have consequently become a major field of struggle through which monopoly powers more generally are asserted. The pharmaceutical industry, to take a paradigmatic example, has acquired extraordinary monopoly powers, in part through massive centralizations of capital and in part through the protection of patents and licensing agreements. And it is hungrily pursuing even more monopoly powers as it seeks to establish property rights over genetic materials of all sorts (including those of rare plants in tropical rainforests traditionally collected by indigenous inhabitants). As monopoly privileges from one source diminish, so we witness a variety of attempts to preserve and assemble them by other means.

I cannot possibly review all of these tendencies here. I do want, however, to look more closely at those aspects of this process that impinge most directly upon the problems of local development and cultural activities. I wish to show, first, that there are continuing struggles over the definition of the monopoly powers that might be accorded to location and localities, and that the idea of "culture" is more and more entangled with attempts to reassert such monopoly powers precisely because claims to uniqueness and authenticity can best be articulated as distinctive and non-replicable cultural claims. I begin with the most obvious example of monopoly rent, given by "the vineyard producing wine of extraordinary quality that can be sold at a monopoly price."

ADVENTURES IN THE WINE TRADE

The wine trade, like brewing, has become more and more international over the last thirty years, and the stresses of international competition have produced some curious effects. Under pressure from the European Union, for example, international wine producers have agreed (after long legal battles and intense negotiations) to phase out the use of "traditional expressions" on wine labels, which could eventually include terms like "château" and "domaine" as well as generic terms like "champagne," "burgundy," "chablis" or "sauterne." In this way the European wine industry, led by the French, seeks to preserve monopoly rents by insisting upon the unique virtues of land, climate, and tradition (lumped together under the French term "terroir") and the distinctiveness of its product certified by a name. Reinforced by institutional controls like "appellation contrôlée," the French wine trade insists upon the authenticity and originality of its product, which grounds the uniqueness upon which monopoly rent can be based.

Australia is one of the countries that agreed to this move. Chateau Tahbilk in Victoria obliged by dropping the "Chateau" from its label, airily pronouncing that "we are proudly Australian with no need to use terms inherited from other countries and cultures of bygone days." To compensate, they identified two factors which, when combined, "give us a unique position in the world of wine." Theirs is one of only six worldwide wine regions where the meso-climate is dramatically influenced by inland water mass (the numerous lakes and local lagoons moderate and cool the climate). Their soil is of a unique type (found in only one other location in Victoria), described as red/sandy loam colored by a very high ferric oxide content, which "has a positive effect on grape quality and adds a certain distinctive regional character to our wines." These two factors are brought together to define "Nagambie Lakes" as a unique Viticultural Region (to be authenticated, presumably, by the Australian Wine and Brandy Corporation's Geographical Indications Committee, set up to identify Viticultural regions throughout Australia). Tahbilk thereby establishes a counter-claim to monopoly rents on the grounds of the unique mix of environmental conditions in the region where it is situated. It does so in a way that parallels and competes with the uniqueness claims of "terroir" and "domaine" pressed by French wine producers.[10]

But we then encounter the first contradiction. All wine is tradable, and therefore in some sense comparable, no matter where it is from. Enter Robert Parker and the *Wine Advocate*, which he publishes regularly. Parker evaluates wines for their taste and pays no particular mind to "terroir" or any other cultural-historical claims. He is notoriously independent (most other guides are supported by influential sectors of the wine industry). He ranks wines on a scale according to his own distinctive taste. He has an extensive following in the United States, a major market. If he rates a Château wine from Bordeaux 65 points and an Australian wine 95 points, then prices are affected. The Bordeaux wine producers are terrified of him. They have sued him, denigrated him, abused him, and even physically assaulted him. He challenges the bases of their monopoly rents.[11]

Monopoly claims, we can conclude, are as much an "effect of discourse" and an outcome of struggle as they are a reflection of the qualities of the product. But if the language of "terroir" and tradition is to be abandoned, then what kind of discourse can be put in its place? Parker and many others in the wine trade have in recent years invented a language in which wines are described in terms such as "flavor of peach and plum, with a hint of thyme and gooseberry." The language sounds bizarre, but this discursive shift, which corresponds to rising international competition and globalization in the wine trade, takes on a distinctive role, reflecting the commodification of wine consumption along standardized lines.

But wine consumption has many dimensions that open paths to profitable exploitation. For many it is an aesthetic experience. Beyond the sheer pleasure (for some) of a fine wine with the right food, there lie all sorts of other referents within the Western tradition that track back to mythology (Dionysus and Bacchus), religion (the blood of Jesus and communion rituals), and traditions celebrated in festivals, poetry, song, and literature. Knowledge of wines and "proper" appreciation are often signs of class, and are analyzable as a form of "cultural" capital (as Bourdieu would put it). Getting the wine right may have helped to seal more than a few major business deals. (Would you trust someone who did not know how to select a wine?) Style of wine is related to regional cuisines, and thereby embedded in those practices that turn regionality into a way of life marked by distinctive structures of feeling (it is hard to imagine Zorba the Greek drinking Mondavi Californian jug wine, even though the latter is sold in Athens airport).

The wine trade is about money and profit, but it is also about culture in all of its senses (from the culture of the product to the cultural practices that surround its consumption and the cultural capital that can evolve alongside it among both producers and consumers). The perpetual search for monopoly rents entails seeking out criteria of specialty, uniqueness, originality, and authenticity in each of these realms. If uniqueness cannot be established by appeal to "terroir" and tradition, or by straight description of flavor, then other modes of distinction must be invoked to establish monopoly claims and discourses devised to guarantee the truth of those claims (the wine that guarantees seduction or the wine that goes with nostalgia and the log fire are current advertising tropes in the United States). In practice, what we find within the wine trade is a host of competing discourses, all with different truth claims about the uniqueness of the product. But, to return to my starting point, all of these discursive shifts and fluxions, as well as many of the shifts and turns that have occurred in the strategies for commanding the international market in wine, have at their root not only the search for profit but also the search for monopoly rents. In this the language of authenticity, originality, uniqueness, and special un-replicable qualities looms large. The generality of a globalized market produces, in a manner consistent with the second contradiction I identified earlier, a powerful force seeking to guarantee not only the continuing monopoly privileges of private property, but the monopoly rents that derive from depicting commodities as incomparable.

URBAN ENTREPRENEURIALISM AND THE SEARCH FOR MONOPOLY RENTS

Recent struggles within the wine trade provide a useful model for understanding a wide range of phenomena within the contemporary phase of globalization. They have particular relevance for understanding how local cultural developments and traditions become absorbed within the calculi of political economy through attempts to garner monopoly rents. They also pose the question of how much the current interest in local cultural innovation and the resurrection and invention of local traditions attaches to the desire to extract and appropriate such rents. Since capitalists of all sorts (including the most exuberant of international financiers) are easily seduced by the lucrative prospects of monopoly powers, we immediately discern a third contradiction: that the most avid globalizers will support local developments that have the potential to yield monopoly rents even if the effect of such support is to produce a local political climate antagonistic to globalization. Emphasizing the uniqueness and purity of local Balinese culture may be vital to the hotel, airline, and tourist industry, but what happens when this encourages a Balinese movement that violently resists the "impurity" of commercialization? The Basque Country may appear a potentially valuable cultural configuration precisely because of its uniqueness, but ETA, with its demand for autonomy and preparedness from time to time to take violent action, is not easily amenable to commercialization. But the lengths to which commercial interests can go are amazing. After the release of the film *City of God*, which depicted the violence and drug wars of Rio's favelas in monstrously (and, some would say, misleading) graphic detail, an enterprising tourist industry started to market favela tours in some of the more dangerous neighborhoods (you could chose your own preferred level of tour risk). Let us probe a little more deeply into this contradiction as it impinges upon urban development politics. In order to do so, however, we must briefly situate those politics in relation to globalization.

Urban entrepreneurialism has become important both nationally and internationally in recent decades. By this I mean that pattern of behavior within urban governance that mixes together state powers (local, metropolitan, regional, national, or supranational) with a wide array of organizational forms in civil society (chambers of commerce, unions, churches, educational and research institutions, community groups, NGOs, and so on) and private interests (corporate and individual) to form coalitions to promote or manage urban or regional development of one sort or another. There is now an extensive literature on this topic which shows that the forms, activities, and goals of these governance systems (variously known as "urban regimes," "growth machines" or "regional growth coalitions") vary widely depending upon local conditions and the mix of forces at work within them.[12] The role of this urban entrepreneurialism in relation to the neoliberal form of globalization has also been scrutinized at length, most usually under the rubric of local-global relations and the so-called "space-place dialectic." Most geographers who have looked into the problem have rightly concluded that it is a categorical error to view globalization as a causal force in relation to local development. What is at stake here, they rightly argue, is a rather more complicated relationship across scales in which local initiatives can percolate upwards to a global scale and vice versa, at the same time as processes within a particular definition of scale—interurban and interregional competition being the most obvious examples—can rework the local and regional configurations of what globalization is about.

Globalization should not be seen, therefore, as an undifferentiated unity, but as a geographically articulated patterning of global capitalist activities and relations.[13] But what, exactly, does it mean to speak of a "geographically articulated patterning"? There is, of course, plenty of evidence of uneven geographical development (at a variety of scales), and at least some cogent theorizing to understand its capitalistic logic. Some of it can be understood in conventional terms as a search on the part of mobile capitals (with financial, commercial, and production capital having different capacities in this regard) to gain advantages in the production and appropriation of surplus values by moving around. Trends can indeed be identified that fit with simple models of a "race to the bottom" in which the cheapest and most easily exploited labor-power becomes the guiding beacon for capital mobility and investment decisions. But there is plenty of countervailing evidence to suggest that this is a gross oversimplification when projected as a monocausal explanation of the dynamics of uneven geographical development. Capital in general just as easily flows into high-wage regions as into low-wage ones, and often seems to be geographically guided by quite different criteria to those conventionally set out in both bourgeois and Marxist political economy.

The problem derives partly from the habit of ignoring the category of landed capital and the considerable importance of long-term investments in the built environment, which are by definition geographically immobile. Such investments, particularly when they are of a speculative sort, invariably invite even further waves of investment if the first wave proves profitable (to fill the convention center we need the hotels, which require better transport and communications, which create the possibility of expanding the capacity of the convention center …). So there is an element of circular and cumulative causation at work in the dynamics of metropolitan area investments (look, for example, at the whole Docklands redevelopment in London and the financial viability of Canary Wharf, which pivots on further investments, both public and private, in the area). This is what so-called "urban growth machines" are often all about: the orchestration of investment process dynamics and the provision of key public investments at the right place and time to promote success in inter-urban and inter-regional competition.[14]

But this would not be as attractive as it is were it not for the ways in which monopoly rents might also be captured. A well-known strategy of developers, for example, is to reserve the choicest and most rentable piece of land in some development in order to extract monopoly rent from it after the rest of the project is realized. Savvy governments with the requisite powers can engage in the same practices. The government of Hong Kong, as I understand it, is largely financed by controlled sales of public domain land for development at very high monopoly prices. This converts, in turn, into monopoly rents on properties, which makes Hong Kong very attractive to international financial investment capital working through property markets. Of course, Hong Kong has other uniqueness claims, given its location, upon which it can also trade very vigorously in offering monopoly advantages. Singapore, incidentally, set out to capture monopoly rents, and was highly successful in so doing in somewhat similar fashion, though by very different political-economic means.

Urban governance of this sort is mostly oriented to constructing patterns of local investments not only in physical infrastructures such as transport and communications, port facilities, sewage, and water, but also in the social infrastructures of education, technology and science, social control, culture, and living quality. The aim is to create sufficient synergy within the urbanization process for monopoly rents to be created and realized by both private interests and state powers. Not all such efforts are successful, of course, but even the unsuccessful examples can partly or largely be understood in terms of their failure to realize monopoly rents. But the search for monopoly rents is not confined to the practices of real estate development, economic initiatives, and government finance. It has a far wider application.

COLLECTIVE SYMBOLIC CAPITAL, MARKS OF DISTINCTION, AND MONOPOLY RENTS

If claims to uniqueness, authenticity, particularity, and specialty underlie the ability to capture monopoly rents, then on what better terrain is it possible to make such claims than in the field of historically constituted cultural artifacts and practices and special environmental characteristics (including, of course, the built, social, and cultural environments)? As in the wine trade, all such claims are as much an outcome of discursive constructions and struggles as they are grounded in material fact. Many rest upon historical narratives, interpretations and meanings of collective memories, significations of cultural practices, and the like: there is always a strong social and discursive element at work in the construction of such causes for extracting monopoly rents, since there will be, at least in many people's minds, no other place than London, Cairo, Barcelona, Milan, Istanbul, San Francisco, or wherever, in which to gain access to whatever it is that is supposedly unique to such places.

The most obvious example is contemporary tourism, but I think it would be a mistake to let the matter rest there. For what is at stake here is the power of collective symbolic capital, of special marks of distinction that attach to some place, which have a significant drawing power upon the flows of capital more generally. Bourdieu, to whom we owe the general usage of these terms, unfortunately restricts them to individuals (rather like atoms floating in a sea of structured aesthetic judgments), when it seems to me that the collective forms (and the relation of individuals to those collective forms) might be of even greater interest.[15]

The collective symbolic capital which attaches to names and places like Paris, Athens, New York, Rio de Janeiro, Berlin, and Rome is of great import and gives such places great economic advantages relative to, say, Baltimore, Liverpool, Essen, Lille, and Glasgow. The problem for these latter places is to raise their quotient of symbolic capital and to increase their marks of distinction so as to better ground their claims to the uniqueness that yields monopoly rent. The "branding" of cities becomes big business.[16] Given the general loss of other monopoly powers through easier transport and communications and the reduction of other barriers to trade, this struggle for collective symbolic capital has become even more important as a basis for monopoly rents. How else can we explain the splash made by the Guggenheim Museum in Bilbao, with its signature Gehry architecture? And how else can we explain the willingness of major financial institutions, with considerable international interests, to finance such a signature project?

The rise to prominence of Barcelona within the European system of cities, to take another example, has in part been based on its steady amassing of symbolic capital and its accumulation of marks of distinction. In this the excavation of a distinctively Catalan history and tradition, the marketing of its strong artistic accomplishments and architectural heritage (Gaudí, of course), and its distinctive marks of lifestyle and literary traditions, have loomed large, backed by a deluge of books, exhibitions, and cultural events that celebrate its distinctiveness. This has all been showcased with new signature architectural embellishments (Norman Foster's radio communications tower and Meier's gleaming white Museum of Modern Art in the midst of the somewhat degraded fabric of the old city) and a whole host of investments to open up the harbor and the beach, reclaim derelict lands for the Olympic Village (with cute reference to the utopianism of the Icarians), and turn what was once a rather murky and even dangerous nightlife into an open panorama of urban spectacle. All of this was helped on by the Olympic Games, which opened up huge opportunities to garner monopoly rents (Samaranch, president of the International Olympic Committee, just happened to have large real estate interests in Barcelona).[17]

But Barcelona's initial success appears to be headed deep into the first contradiction. As opportunities to pocket monopoly rents galore present themselves on the basis of the collective symbolic capital of Barcelona as a city (property prices have skyrocketed since the Royal Institute of British Architects awarded the whole city its medal for architectural accomplishments), so their irresistible lure draws more and more homogenizing multinational commodification in its wake. The later phases of waterfront development look exactly like every other in the western world: the stupefying congestion of the traffic leads to pressures to put boulevards through parts of the old city, multinational stores replace local shops, gentrification removes long-term residential populations and destroys older urban fabric, and Barcelona loses some of its marks of distinction. There are even unsubtle signs of Disneyfication.

This contradiction is marked by questions and resistance. Whose collective memory is to be celebrated here—the anarchists, like the Icarians, who played such an important role in Barcelona's history; the republicans who fought so fiercely against Franco; the Catalan nationalists, immigrants from Andalusia; or a long-time Franco ally like Samaranch? Whose aesthetics really count—the famously powerful architects of Barcelona, like Bohigas? Why accept Disneyfication of any sort? Debates of this sort cannot easily be stilled precisely because it is clear to all that the collective symbolic capital that Barcelona has accumulated depends upon values of authenticity, uniqueness, and particular non-replicable qualities. Such marks of local distinction are hard to accumulate without raising the issue of local empowerment, even of popular and oppositional movements. At that point, of course, the guardians of collective symbolic and cultural capital—the museums, the universities, the class of benefactors, and the state apparatus—typically close their doors and insist upon keeping the riff-raff out (though in Barcelona the Museum of Modern Art, unlike most institutions of its kind, has remained amazingly and constructively open to popular sensibilities). And if that fails, then the state can step in with anything from something like the "decency committee" set up by Mayor Giuliani to monitor cultural taste in New York City to outright police repression. Nevertheless, the stakes here are significant. It is a matter of determining which segments of the population are to benefit most from the collective symbolic capital to which everyone has, in their own distinctive ways, contributed both now and in the past. Why let the monopoly rent attached to that symbolic capital be captured only by the multinationals, or by a small, powerful segment of the local bourgeoisie? Even Singapore, which created and appropriated monopoly rents so ruthlessly and so successfully over the years (mainly out of its locational and positional advantage), saw to it that the benefits were widely distributed through housing, health care and education.

For the sorts of reasons that the recent history of Barcelona exemplifies, the knowledge and heritage industries, the vitality and ferment of cultural production, signature architecture and the cultivation of distinctive aesthetic judgments have become powerful constitutive elements in the politics of urban entrepreneurialism in many places (particularly Europe). The struggle is on to accumulate marks of distinction and collective symbolic capital in a highly competitive world. But this brings in its wake all of the localized questions about whose collective memory, whose aesthetics, and whose benefits are to be prioritized. Neighborhood movements in Barcelona make claims for recognition and empowerment on the basis of symbolic capital, and can assert a political presence in the city as a result. It is their urban commons that are appropriated all too often not only by developers, but by the tourist trade. But the selective nature of such appropriations can mobilize further new avenues of political struggle. The initial erasure of all mention of the slave trade in the reconstruction of Albert Dock in Liverpool generated protests on the part of the excluded population of Caribbean background, and produced new political solidarities among a marginalized population. The holocaust memorial in Berlin has sparked long-drawn-out controversies. Even ancient monuments such as the Acropolis, whose meaning one would have thought by now would be well-settled, are subject to contestation.[18] Such contestations can have widespread, even if indirect, political implications. The popular production of a new urban commons, the amassing of collective symbolic capital, the mobilization of collective memories and mythologies, and appeals to specific cultural traditions are important facets of all forms of political action, of both left and right.

Consider, for example, the arguments that swirled around the reconstruction of Berlin after German reunification. All manner of divergent forces collided there as the struggle to define Berlin's symbolic capital unfolded. Berlin, rather obviously, can stake a claim to uniqueness on the basis of its potential to mediate between east and west. Its strategic

position in relation to the uneven geographical development of contemporary capitalism (with the opening up of the former Soviet Union)
confers obvious advantages. But there is also another kind of battle for
identity being waged which invokes collective memories, mythologies,
history, culture, aesthetics, and tradition. I take up just one particularly
troubling dimension of this struggle—one that is not necessarily dominant, and whose capacity to ground claims to monopoly rent under
global competition is not at all clear or certain. A faction of local architects and planners (with the support of certain parts of the local state
apparatus) sought to revalidate the architectural forms of eighteenth- and
nineteenth-century Berlin, and in particular to highlight the architectural tradition of Schinkel, to the exclusion of much else. This might be
seen as a simple matter of elitist aesthetic preference, but it is freighted
with a whole range of meanings that have to do with collective memories,
monumentality, the power of history, and political identity in the city. It
is also associated with that climate of opinion (articulated in a variety of
discourses) which defines who is or is not a Berliner, and who has a right
to the city in narrowly defined terms of pedigree or adherence to particular values and beliefs. It excavates a local history and an architectural
heritage that is charged with nationalist and romanticist connotations.
In a context where the ill-treatment of and violence against immigrants
is widespread, it may even offer tacit legitimation to such actions. The
Turkish population, many of whom are now Berlin-born, have suf-
fered many indignities, and have largely been forced out from the city
center. Their contribution to Berlin as a city is ignored. Furthermore, the
romanticist/nationalist architectural style fits with a traditional approach
to monumentality that broadly replicates in contemporary plans (though
without specific reference, and maybe even unknowingly) Albert Speer's
plans, drawn up for Hitler in the 1930s, for a monumental foreground to
the Reichstag.

This is not, fortunately, all that is going on in the search for collective symbolic capital in Berlin. Norman Foster's reconstruction of
the Reichstag, for example, or the collection of international modernist architects brought in by the multinationals (largely in opposition to
local architects) to dominate the Potsdamer Platz, are hardly consistent
with it. And the local romanticist response to the threat of multinational

domination could, of course, merely end up being an innocent element of interest in a complex achievement of diverse marks of distinction for the city (Schinkel, after all, has considerable architectural merit, and a rebuilt eighteenth-century castle could easily lend itself to Disneyfication).

But the potential downside of the story is of interest because it highlights how the contradictions of monopoly rent can all too easily play out. Were these narrower plans and exclusionary aesthetics and discursive practices to become dominant, then the collective symbolic capital created would be hard to trade freely upon, because its very special qualities would position it largely outside globalization and inside an exclusionary political culture that rejects much of what globalization is about, turning inward towards a parochial nationalism at best and a virulent rejection of foreigners and immigrants at worst. The collective monopoly powers that urban governance can command can be directed towards opposition to the banal cosmopolitanism of multinational globalization, but thereby ground localized nationalism. The cultural terms in which aid to the Greeks to deal with their indebtedness was widely rejected in the court of German public opinion suggests that the fostering of such localist nationalism can have serious global consequences. The successful branding of a city may require the expulsion or eradication of everyone or everything else that does not fit the brand.

The dilemma—between veering so close to pure commercialization as to lose the marks of distinction that underlie monopoly rents, or constructing marks of distinction that are so special as to be very hard to trade upon—is perpetually present. But, as in the wine trade, there are always strong discursive gambits involved in defining what is or is not so special about a product, a place, a cultural form, a tradition, an architectural heritage. Discursive battles become part of the game, and advocates (in the media and academia, for example) gain their audience as well as their financial support in relation to these processes. There is much to achieve, for example, by appeals to fashion (interestingly, being a center of fashion is one way for cities to accumulate considerable collective symbolic capital). Capitalists are well aware of this, and must therefore wade into the culture wars, as well as into the thickets of multiculturalism, fashion, and aesthetics, because it is precisely through such means that monopoly rents stand to be gained, if only for a while. And if, as I claim, monopoly rent is always an object of capitalist desire, then the means of gaining it through interventions in the field of culture, history, heritage, aesthetics, and meanings must necessarily be of great import for capitalists of any sort. The question then arises as to how these cultural interventions can themselves become a potent weapon of class struggle.

MONOPOLY RENT AND SPACES OF HOPE

By now critics will complain at the seeming economic reductionism of the argument. I make it seem, they will say, as if capitalism produces local cultures, shapes aesthetic meanings, and so dominates local initiatives as to preclude the development of any kind of difference that is not directly subsumed within the circulation of capital. I cannot prevent such a reading, but this would be a perversion of my message. For what I hope to have shown by invoking the concept of monopoly rent within the logic of capital accumulation is that capital has ways to appropriate and extract surpluses from local differences, local cultural variations, and aesthetic meanings of no matter what origin. European tourists can now enjoy commercialized tours of New York's Harlem (with a gospel choir thrown in), just as "poverty tourism" touts trips to zones of intense poverty in the shanty-towns of South Africa, Dharavi in Mumbai, and the favelas of Rio. The music industry in the United States succeeds brilliantly in appropriating the incredible grassroots and localized creativity of musicians of all stripes (almost invariably to the benefit of the industry rather than the musicians). Even politically explicit music which speaks to the long history of oppression (including some forms of rap, Jamaican reggae, and Kingston Dance Hall music) becomes commodified. The commodification and commercialization of everything is, after all, one of the hallmarks of our times.

But monopoly rent is a contradictory form. The search for it leads global capital to value distinctive local initiatives—indeed, in certain respects, the more distinctive and, in these times, the more transgressive the initiative, the better. It also leads to the valuation of uniqueness, authenticity, particularity, originality, and all manner of other dimensions to social life that are inconsistent with the homogeneity presupposed by commodity production. And if capital is not to totally destroy the uniqueness that is the basis for the appropriation of monopoly rents (and there are many circumstances where it has done just that and been roundly condemned for so doing), then it must support a form of differentiation and allow of divergent and to some degree uncontrollable local cultural developments that can be antagonistic to its own smooth functioning. It can even support (though cautiously and often nervously) transgressive cultural practices precisely because this is one way in which to be original, creative, and authentic, as well as unique.

It is within such spaces that oppositional movements can form, even presupposing, as is often the case, that oppositional movements are not already firmly entrenched there. The problem for capital is to find ways to co-opt, subsume, commodify, and monetize such cultural differences and cultural commons just enough to be able to appropriate monopoly rents from them. In so doing, capital often produces widespread alienation and resentment among the cultural producers who experience first-hand the appropriation and exploitation of their creativity and their political commitments for the economic benefit of others, in much the same way that whole populations can resent having their histories and cultures exploited through commodification. The problem for oppositional movements is to speak to this widespread appropriation of their cultural commons and to use the validation of particularity, uniqueness, authenticity, culture, and aesthetic meanings in ways that open up new possibilities and alternatives.

At the very minimum, this means resistance to the idea that authenticity, creativity, and originality are an exclusive product of bourgeois rather than working-class, peasant, or other non-capitalistic historical geographies. It also entails trying to persuade contemporary cultural producers to redirect their anger towards commodification, market domination, and the capitalistic system more generally. It is, for example, one thing to be transgressive about sexuality, religion, social mores, and artistic and architectural conventions, but quite another to be transgressive in relation to the institutions and practices of capitalist domination that actually penetrate deeply into cultural institutions. The widespread though usually fragmented struggles that exist between capitalistic appropriation and past and present cultural creativity can lead a segment of the community concerned with cultural matters to side with a politics opposed to multinational capitalism and in favor of some more compelling alternative based on different kinds of social and ecological relations. This does not mean that attachment to "pure" values of authenticity, originality, and an aesthetic of particularity of culture is an adequate foundation for a progressive oppositional politics. It can all too easily veer into local, regional, or nationalist identity politics of the neofascist sort, of which there are already far too many troubling signs throughout much of Europe, as well as elsewhere. This is a central contradiction with which the left must wrestle. The spaces for transformational politics are there because capital can never afford to close them down. They provide opportunities for socialist opposition. They can be the locus of exploration of alternative lifestyles, or even of social philosophies (much as Curitiba in Brazil has pioneered ideas of urban ecological sustainability to the point of reaping considerable fame from its initiatives). They can, like the Paris Commune of 1871 or the numerous urban-based political movements around the world in 1968, be a central element in that revolutionary ferment that Lenin long ago called "the festival of the people." The fragmented oppositional movements to neoliberal globalization, as manifest in Seattle, Prague, Melbourne, Bangkok, and Nice, and then more constructively as the 2001 World Social Forum in Porto Alegre, indicate such an alternative politics. It is not wholly antagonistic to globalization, but wants it on very different terms. The striving for a certain kind of cultural autonomy and support for cultural creativity and differentiation is a powerful constitutive element in these political movements.

It is no accident, of course, that it is Porto Alegre rather than Barcelona, Berlin, San Francisco, or Milan, that has opened itself to such oppositional initiatives.[19] For in that city the forces of culture and of history are being mobilized by a political movement (led by the Brazilian Workers' Party) in a quite different way, seeking a different kind of collective symbolic capital to that flaunted in the Guggenheim Museum in Bilbao or the extension to the Tate Gallery in London. The marks of distinction being accumulated in Porto Alegre derive from its struggle to fashion an alternative to globalization that does not trade on monopoly rents in particular or cave in to multinational capitalism in general. In focusing on popular mobilization, it is actively constructing new cultural forms and new definitions of authenticity, originality, and tradition. That is a hard path to follow, as was shown by previous examples, such as the remarkable experiments in Red Bologna in the 1960s and 1970s. Socialism in one city is not a viable concept, but it is in the cities that the conditions for both the production and appropriation of monopoly rents are most highly concentrated, in terms of both physical investments and cultural movements. No alternative to the contemporary form of globalization will be delivered to us from on high. It will have to come from within multiple local spaces—urban spaces in particular—conjoining into a broader movement. It is here that the contradictions faced by capitalists as they search for monopoly rent assume a certain structural significance. By seeking to trade on values of authenticity, locality, history, culture, collective memories, and tradition they open a space for political thought and action within which socialist alternatives can be both devised and pursued. The space of that commons deserves intense exploration and cultivation by oppositional movements that embrace cultural producers and cultural production as a key element in their political strategy. There are abundant historical precedents for mobilizing the forces of high culture in this way (the role of constructivism in the creative years of the Russian Revolution from 1918 to 1926 is just one of many instructive historical examples). But popular culture as produced through the common relationships of daily life is also crucial. Here lies one of the key spaces of hope for the construction of an alternative kind of globalization and a vibrant anti-commodification politics: one in which the progressive forces of cultural production and transformation can seek to appropriate and undermine the forces of capital rather than the other way round.

Section II:
Rebel Cities

CHAPTER FIVE

Reclaiming the City for Anti-Capitalist Struggle

If urbanization is so crucial in the history of capital accumulation, and if the forces of capital and its innumerable allies must relentlessly mobilize to periodically revolutionize urban life, then class struggles of some sort, no matter whether they are explicitly recognized as such, are inevitably involved. This is so if only because the forces of capital have to struggle mightily to impose their will on an urban process and whole populations that can never, even under the most favorable of circumstances, be under their total control. An important strategic political question then follows: To what degree should anti-capitalist struggles explicitly focus and organize on the broad terrain of the city and the urban? And if they should do so, then how and exactly why?

The history of urban-based class struggles is stunning. The successive revolutionary movements in Paris from 1789 through 1830 and 1848 to the Commune of 1871 constitute the most obvious nineteenth-century example. Later events included the Petrograd Soviet, the Shanghai Communes of 1927 and 1967, the Seattle General Strike of 1919, the role of Barcelona in the Spanish Civil War, the uprising in Córdoba in 1969, and the more general urban uprisings in the United States in the 1960s, the urban-based movements of 1968 (Paris, Chicago, Mexico City, Bangkok, and others including the so-called "Prague Spring," and the rise of neighborhood associations in Madrid that fronted the anti-Franco movement in Spain around the same time). And in more recent times we have witnessed echoes of these older struggles in the Seattle anti-globalization protests of 1999 (followed by similar protests in Quebec City, Genoa, and many other cities as part of a widespread alternative globalization movement). Most recently we have seen mass protests in Tahrir Square in Cairo, in Madison, Wisconsin, in the Plazas del Sol in Madrid and Catalunya in Barcelona, and in Syntagma Square in Athens, as well as revolutionary movements and rebellions in Oaxaca in Mexico, in Cochabamba (2000 and 2007) and El Alto (2003 and 2005) in Bolivia, along with very different but equally important political eruptions in Buenos Aires in 2001–02, and in Santiago in Chile (2006 and 2011).

And it is not, this history demonstrates, only singular urban centers that are involved. On several occasions the spirit of protest and revolt has spread contagiously through urban networks in remarkable ways. The revolutionary movement of 1848 may have started in Paris, but the spirit of revolt spread to Vienna, Berlin, Milan, Budapest, Frankfurt, and many other European cities. The Bolshevik Revolution in Russia was accompanied by the formation of worker's councils and "soviets" in Berlin, Vienna, Warsaw, Riga, Munich and Turin, just as in 1968 it was Paris, Berlin, London, Mexico City, Bangkok, Chicago, and innumerable other cities that experienced "days of rage," and in some instances violent repressions. The unfolding urban crisis of the 1960s in the United States affected many cities simultaneously. And in an astonishing but much-underestimated moment in world history, on February 15, 2003, several million people simultaneously appeared on the streets of Rome (with around 3 million, considered the largest anti-war rally ever in human history), Madrid, London, Barcelona, Berlin, and Athens, with lesser but still substantial numbers (though impossible to count because of police repression) in New York and Melbourne, and thousands more in nearly 200 cities in Asia (except China), Africa, and Latin America in a world-wide demonstration against the threat of war with Iraq. Described at the time as perhaps one of the first expressions of global public opinion, the movement quickly faded, but leaves behind the sense that the global urban network is replete with political possibilities that remain untapped by progressive movements. The current wave of youth-led movements throughout the world, from Cairo to Madrid to Santiago—to say nothing of a street revolt in London, followed by an "Occupy Wall Street" movement that began in New York City before spreading to innumerable cities in the US and now around the world—suggests there is something political in the city air struggling to be expressed.[1]

Two questions derive from this brief account of urban-based political movements. Is the city (or a system of cities) merely a passive site (or pre-existing network)—the place of appearance—where deeper currents of political struggle are expressed? On the surface it might seem so. Yet it is also clear that certain urban environmental characteristics are more conducive to rebellious protests than others—such as the centrality of squares like Tahrir, Tiananmen, and Syntagma, the more easily barricaded streets of Paris compared to London or Los Angeles, or El Alto's position commanding the main supply routes into La Paz.

Political power therefore often seeks to reorganize urban infrastructures and urban life with an eye to the control of restive populations. This was most famously the case with Haussmann's boulevards in Paris, which were viewed even at the time as a means of military control of rebellious citizens. This case is not unique. The re-engineering of inner cities in the United States in the wake of the urban uprisings of the 1960s just happened to create major physical highway barriers—moats, in effect—between the citadels of high-value downtown property and impoverished inner-city neighborhoods. The violent struggles that occurred in the drive to subdue oppositional movements in Ramallah on the West Bank (pursued by the Israeli IDF) and Fallujah in Iraq (pursued by the US military) have played a crucial role in forcing a re-think of military strategies to pacify, police, and control urban populations. Oppositional movements like Hezbollah and Hamas, in their turn, increasingly pursue urbanized strategies of revolt. Militarization is not, of course, the only solution (and, as Fallujah demonstrated, it may be far from the best). The planned pacification programs in Rio's favelas entail an urbanized approach to social and class warfare through the application of a range of different public policies to troubled neighborhoods. For their part, Hezbollah and Hamas both combine military operations from within the dense networks of urban environments with the construction of alternative urban governance structures, incorporating everything from garbage removal to social support payments and neighborhood administrations.

The urban obviously functions, then, as an important site of political action and revolt. The actual site characteristics are important, and the physical and social re-engineering and territorial organization of these sites is a weapon in political struggles. In the same way that, in military operations, the choice and shaping of the terrain of action plays an important role in determining who wins, so it is with popular protests and political movements in urban settings.[2]

The second major point is that political protests frequently gauge their effectiveness in terms of their ability to disrupt urban economies. In the spring of 2006, for example, widespread agitation developed in the United States within immigrant populations over a proposal before Congress to criminalize undocumented immigrants (some of whom had been in the country for decades). The massive protests amounted to what was in effect an immigrant workers' strike that effectively closed down economic activity in Los Angeles and Chicago, and had serious impacts on other cities as well. This impressive demonstration of the political and economic power of unorganized immigrants (both legal and illegal) to disrupt the flows of production as well as the flows of goods and services in major urban centers played an important role in stopping the proposed legislation.

The immigrants' rights movement arose out of nowhere, and was marked by a good deal of spontaneity. But it then fell off rapidly, leaving behind two minor but perhaps significant achievements, in addition to blocking the proposed legislation: the formation of a permanent immigrant workers' alliance and a new tradition in the United States of celebrating May Day as a day to march in support of the aspirations of labor. While this last achievement appears purely symbolic, it nevertheless reminds the unorganized as well as the organized workers in the United States of their collective potentiality. One of the main barriers to the realization of this potentiality also became clear in the rapid decline of the movement. Largely Hispanic-based, it failed to negotiate effectively with the leadership of the African-American population. This opened the way for an intense barrage of propaganda orchestrated by the right-wing media, which suddenly shed crocodile tears for how African-American jobs were being taken away by illegal Hispanic immigrants.[3]

The rapidity and volatility with which massive protest movements have risen and fallen over the last few decades calls for some commentary. In addition to the global anti-war demonstration of 2003 and the rise and fall of the immigrant workers' rights movement in the United States in 2006, there are innumerable examples of the erratic track and uneven geographical expression of oppositional movements; they include the rapidity with which the revolts in the French suburbs in 2005 and the revolutionary bursts in much of Latin America, from Argentina in 2001–02 to Bolivia in 2000–05, were controlled and reabsorbed into dominant capitalist practices. Will the populist protests of the *indignados* throughout southern Europe in 2011, and the more recent Occupy Wall Street movement, have staying power? Understanding the politics and revolutionary potential of such movements is a serious challenge. The fluctuating history and fortunes of the anti- or alternative globalization movement since the late 1990s also suggests that we are in a very particular and perhaps radically different phase of anti-capitalist struggle. Formalized through the World Social Forum and its regional offshoots, and increasingly ritualized as periodic demonstrations against the World Bank, the IMF, the G7 (now the G20), or at almost any international meeting on any issue (from climate change to racism and gender equality), this movement is hard to pin down because it is "a movement of movements" rather than a single-minded organization.[4] It is not that traditional forms of left organizing (left political parties and militant sects, labor unions and militant environmental or social movements such as the Maoists in India or the landless peasants movement in Brazil) have disappeared. But they now all seem to swim within an ocean of more diffuse oppositional movements that lack overall political coherence.

CHANGING LEFT PERSPECTIVES ON ANTI-CAPITALIST STRUGGLES

The bigger question I wish to address here is this: Are the urban manifestations of all these diverse movements anything other than mere side-effects of global, cosmopolitan, or even universal human aspirations that have nothing specifically to do with the particularities of urban life? Or is there something about the urban process and the urban experience —the qualities of daily urban life—under capitalism that, *in itself*, has the potential to ground anti-capitalist struggles? If so, then what constitutes this grounding and how can it be mobilized and put to use to challenge the dominant political and economic powers of capital, along with its hegemonic ideological practices and its powerful grasp upon political subjectivities (this last point is, in my view, critical)? In other words, should struggles within and over the city, and over the qualities and prospects of urban living, be seen as fundamental to anti-capitalist politics?

I do not claim here that the answer to this question is "obviously yes." I do claim, however, that this question is inherently worth asking.

For many on the traditional left (by which I mainly mean socialist and communist political parties and most trade unions), the interpretation of the historical geography of urban-based political movements has been dogged by political and tactical a priori assumptions that have led to the underestimation and misunderstanding of the potency of urban-based movements for sparking not only radical but also revolutionary change. Urban social movements are all too often viewed as by definition separate from or ancillary to those class and anti-capitalist struggles that have their roots in the exploitation and alienation of living labor in production. If urban social movements are considered at all, they are typically construed as either mere offshoots or displacements of these more fundamental struggles. Within the Marxist tradition, for example, urban struggles tend to be either ignored or dismissed as devoid of revolutionary potential or significance. Such struggles are construed as being either about issues of reproduction rather than production, or about rights, sovereignty, and citizenship, and therefore not about class. The immigrant workers' movement of unorganized labor in 2006, the argument goes, was basically about claiming rights and not about revolution.

When a city-wide struggle does acquire an iconic revolutionary status, as in the case of the Paris Commune of 1871, it is claimed (first by Marx, and even more emphatically by Lenin) as a "proletarian uprising"[5] rather than as a much more complicated revolutionary movement—animated as much by the desire to reclaim the city itself from its bourgeois appropriation as by the desired liberation of workers from the travails of class oppression in the workplace. I take it as symbolic that the first two acts of the Paris Commune were to abolish night-work in the bakeries (a labor question) and to impose a moratorium on rents (an urban question).

Traditional left groups can therefore on occasion take up urban-based struggles, and when they do they can often be successful even as they seek to interpret their struggle from within their traditional workerist perspective. The British Socialist Workers' Party, for example, led the successful struggle against Thatcher's poll tax in the 1980s (a reform of local government finance that hit the less affluent very hard). Thatcher's defeat on the poll tax almost certainly played a significant role in her downfall.

Anti-capitalist struggle, in the formal Marxist sense, is fundamentally and quite properly construed to be about the abolition of that class relation between capital and labor in production that permits the production and appropriation of surplus value by capital. The ultimate aim of anti-capitalist struggle is the abolition of that class relation and all that goes with it, no matter where it occurs. On the surface, this revolutionary aim seems to have nothing to do with urbanization per se. Even when this struggle has to be seen, as it invariably does, through the prisms of race, ethnicity, sexuality, and gender, and even when it unfolds through urban-based inter-ethnic, racialized, and gendered conflicts within the living spaces of the city, the fundamental conception is that an anti-capitalist struggle must ultimately reach deep into the very guts of what a capitalist system is about and wrench out the cancerous tumor of class relations in production.

It would be a truthful caricature to say that working-class movements in general have long privileged the industrial workers of the world as the vanguard agent in this mission. In Marxist revolutionary versions, this vanguard leads the class struggle through the dictatorship of the proletariat to a promised world where state and class wither away. It is also a truthful caricature to say that things have never worked out this way.

Marx argued that the class relation of domination in production had to be displaced by the associated workers controlling their own production processes and protocols. This view parallels a long history of political pursuit of worker control, *autogestión* (usually translated as "self-management"), worker cooperatives, and the like.[6] These struggles did not necessarily arise out of any conscious attempt to follow Marx's theoretical prescriptions (indeed, the latter almost certainly reflected the former), nor were they necessarily construed in practice as some way-station on the journey to a root-and-branch revolutionary reconstruction of the social order. They more usually arose out of the basic intuition, arrived at in many different places and times by workers themselves, that it would be much fairer, less repressive, and more in accord with their own sense of self-worth and personal dignity to regulate their own social relations and production activities, rather than to submit to the oppressive dictates of an often despotic boss demanding that they give unstintingly of their capacity for alienated labor. But attempts to change the world by worker control and analogous movements—such as community-owned projects, so-called "moral" or "solidarity" economies, local economic trading systems and barter, the creation of autonomous spaces (the most famous of which today would be that of the Zapatistas)—have not so far proved viable as templates for more global anti-capitalist solutions, in spite of the noble efforts and sacrifices that have often kept these efforts going in the face of fierce hostilities and active repressions.[7]

The main reason for the long-run failure of such initiatives to aggregate into some global alternative to capitalism is simple enough. All enterprises operating in a capitalist economy are subject to "the coercive laws of competition" that undergird the capitalist laws of value production and realization. If somebody makes a similar product to me at a lower cost, then I either go out of business, or adapt my production practices to increase my productivity, or lower my costs of labor, intermediate goods and raw materials. While small and localized enterprises can work under the radar and beyond the reach of the laws of competition (acquiring the status of local monopolies, for example), most cannot. So worker-controlled or cooperative enterprises tend at some point to mimic their capitalistic competitors, and the more they do so the less distinctive their practices become. Indeed, it can all too easily happen that workers end up in a condition of collective self-exploitation that is every bit as repressive as that which capital imposes.

Furthermore, as Marx also shows in the second volume of *Capital*, the circulation of capital comprises three distinctive circulatory processes, those of money, productive, and commodity capitals.[8] No one circulatory process can survive or even exist without the others: they intermingle and co-determine each other. Workers' control or community collectives in relatively isolated production units can rarely survive—in spite of all the hopeful *autonomista*, *autogestion* and anarchist rhetoric—in the face of a hostile financial environment and credit system and the predatory practices of merchant capital. The power of finance capital and of merchant capital (the Wal-Mart phenomenon) has been particularly resurgent in recent years (this is a much-neglected topic in contemporary left theorizing). What to do about these other circulation processes and the class forces that crystallize around them thus becomes a large part of the problem. These are, after all, the primal forces through which the iron law of capitalist value determination operates.

The theoretical conclusion that follows is glaringly obvious. The abolition of the class relation in production is contingent upon the abolition of the powers of the capitalist law of value to dictate conditions of production through free trade on the world market. Anti-capitalist struggle must not only be about organizing and re-organizing within the labor process, fundamental though that is. It must also be about finding a political and social alternative to the operation of the capitalist law of value across the world market. While worker control or communitarian movements can arise out of the concrete intuitions of people collectively engaging in production and consumption, contesting the operations of the capitalist law of value on the world stage requires a theoretical understanding of macroeconomic interrelations along with a different form of technical and organizational sophistication. This poses the difficult problem of developing a political and organizational ability both to mobilize and to control the organization of international divisions of labor and of exchange practices and relations on the world market. De-coupling from these relations, as some now propose, is close to impossible for a variety of reasons. Firstly, de-coupling increases the vulnerability to local famines and social and so-called natural catastrophes. Secondly, effective management and survival almost always depends upon the availability of sophisticated means of production. For example, the ability to coordinate flows throughout a commodity chain to a workers' collective (from raw materials to finished products) depends on the availability of power sources and technologies, such as electricity, cell phones, computers, and the internet, that are procured from that world in which the capitalist laws of value creation and circulation predominate.

In the face of these obvious difficulties, many forces on the traditional left turned historically to the conquest of state power as their prime objective. Those powers could then be used to regulate and control capital and money flows, to institute non-market (and non-commodified) systems of exchange through rational planning, and to set in place an alternative to the capitalist laws of value determination through organized and consciously planned reconstructions of the international division of labor. Unable to make this system work globally, communist countries from the Russian Revolution onwards chose to isolate themselves from the capitalist world market as much as possible. The end of the Cold War, the collapse of the Soviet Empire, and the transformation of China into an economy that fully and victoriously embraced the capitalist law of value has resulted in an across-the-board dismissal of this particular anti-capitalist strategy as a feasible path towards building socialism. The centrally planned and even social-democratic idea that the state could even protect against the forces of the world market through protectionism, import substitution (as in Latin America in the 1960s, for example), fiscal policies, and social welfare arrangements, was abandoned step by step as the neoliberal counter-revolutionary movements gathered steam to dominate state apparatuses from the mid 1970s onwards.[9] ✗

The rather dismal historical experience of centrally planned Stalinism and communism as it was actually practiced, and the ultimate failure of social-democratic reformism and protectionism to resist the growing power of capital to control the state and to dictate its policies, has led much of the contemporary left to conclude either that the "smashing of the state" is a necessary precursor to revolutionary transformation or that organizing production autonomously from within the state is the only viable path towards revolutionary change. The burden of politics thus shifts back to some form of worker, community, or localized control. The assumption is that the oppressive power of the state can be "withered away" as oppositional movements of various sorts—factory occupations, solidarity economies, collective autonomous movements, agrarian cooperatives, and the like—gather momentum within civil society. This amounts to what one might call a "termite theory" of revolutionary change: eating away at the institutional and material supports of capital until they collapse. This is not a dismissive term. Termites can inflict terrible damage, often hidden from easy detection. The problem is not lack of potential effectiveness; it is that, as soon as the damage wrought becomes too obvious and threatening, then capital is both able and all too willing to call in the exterminators (state powers) to deal with it. The only hope then is that the exterminators will either turn upon their masters (as they have sometimes done in the past) or be defeated—a rather unlikely outcome except in particular circumstances such as those in Afghanistan—in the course of a militarized struggle. There is, alas, no guarantee that the form of society that will then emerge will be less barbaric than that which it replaces.

Opinions across the broad spectrum of the left on what will work and how are fiercely held, and equally fiercely defended (oftentimes rigidly and dogmatically). To challenge any one particular way of thinking and acting often provokes vituperative responses. The left as a whole is bedeviled by an all-consuming "fetishism of organizational form." The traditional left (communist and socialist in orientation) typically espoused and defended some version of democratic centralism (in political parties, trade unions, and the like). Now, however, principles are frequently advanced—such as "horizontality" and "non-hierarchy"—or visions of radical democracy and the governance of the commons, that can work for small groups but are impossible to operationalize at the scale of a metropolitan region, let alone for the 7 billion people who now inhabit planet earth. Programmatic priorities are dogmatically articulated, such as the abolition of the state, as if no alternative form of territorial governance would ever be necessary or valuable. Even the venerable social anarchist and anti-statist Murray Bookchin, with his theory of confederalism, vigorously advocates the need for some territorial governance, without which the Zapatistas, just to take one recent example, would also certainly have met with death and defeat: though often falsely represented as being totally non-hierachical and "horizontalist" in their organizational structure, the Zapatistas do make decisions through democratically selected delegates and officers.[10] Other groups focus their efforts on the recuperation of ancient and indigenous notions of the rights of nature, or insist that issues of gender, racism, anti-colonialism, or indigeneity must be prioritized above, if not preclude, the pursuit of an anti-capitalist politics. All of this conflicts with the dominant self-perception within these social movements, which tends to believe that there is no guiding or overarching organizational theory, but simply a set of intuitive and flexible practices that arise "naturally" out of given situations. In this, as we shall see, they are not entirely wrong.

To top it all, there is a conspicuous absence of broadly agreed concrete proposals as to how to reorganize divisions of labor and (monetized?) economic transactions throughout the world to sustain a reasonable standard of living for all. Indeed, this problem is all too often cavalierly evaded. As a leading anarchist thinker, David Graeber, puts it, echoing the reservations of Murray Bookchin set out above:

> Temporary bubbles of autonomy must gradually turn into permanent, free communities. However, in order to do so, those communities cannot exist in total isolation; neither can they have a purely confrontational relation with everyone around them. They have to have some way to engage with larger economic, social or political systems that surround them. This is the trickiest question because it has proved extremely difficult for those organized on radically democratic lines to so integrate themselves in any meaningful way in larger structures without having to make endless compromises in their founding principles.[11]

At this point in history, the chaotic processes of capitalist creative destruction have evidently reduced the collective left to a state of energetic but fragmented incoherence, even as periodic eruptions of mass movements of protest and the gnawing threat of "termite politics" suggest that the objective conditions for a more radical break with the capitalist law of value are more than ripe for the taking.

At the heart of all this, however, lies a simple structural dilemma: How can the left fuse the need to actively engage with, but also create an alternative to, the capitalist laws of value determination on the world market, while facilitating the associated laborers' ability democratically and collectively to manage and decide on what they will produce and how? This is the central dialectical tension that has hitherto escaped the ambitious grasp of anti-capitalist alternative movements.[12]

ALTERNATIVES

If a viable anti-capitalist movement is to emerge, then past and current anti-capitalist strategies have to be re-evaluated. Not only is it vital to step back and think about what can and must be done, and who is going to do it where. It is also vital to match preferred organizational principles and practices with the nature of the political, social, and technical battles that have to be fought and won. Whatever solutions, formulations, organizational forms, and political agendas are proposed must provide answers to three compelling questions:

1) The first is that of crushing material impoverishment for much of the world's population, along with the concomitant frustration of the potential for the full development of human capacities and creative powers. Marx was above all a pre-eminent philosopher of human flourishing, but he recognized that this was possible only in "that realm of freedom which begins when the realm of necessity is left behind." The problems of the global accumulation of poverty cannot be confronted, it should be obvious, without confronting the obscene global accumulation of wealth. Anti-poverty organizations need to commit to an anti-wealth politics and to the construction of alternative social relations to those that dominate within capitalism.

2) The second question derives from the clear and imminent dangers of out-of-control environmental degradations and ecological transformations. This, too, is not only a material but also a spiritual and moral question of changing the human sense of nature, as well as the material relation to it. There is no purely technological fix to this question. There have to be significant lifestyle changes (such as rolling back the political, economic, and environmental impacts of the last seventy years of suburbanization) as well as major shifts in consumerism, productivism, and institutional arrangements.

3) The third set of questions, which underpins the first two, derives from a historical and theoretical understanding of the inevitable trajectory of capitalist growth. For a variety of reasons, compounding growth is an

absolute condition for the continuous accumulation and reproduction of capital. This is the socially constructed and historically specific law of endless capital accumulation that has to be challenged and eventually abolished. Compound growth (say, at a minimum of 3 percent forever) is a sheer impossibility. Capital has now arrived at an inflection point (which is different from an impasse) in its long history, where this immanent impossibility is beginning to be realized. Any anti-capitalist alternative has to abolish the power of the capitalist law of value to regulate the world market. This requires the abolition of the dominant class relation that underpins and mandates the perpetual expansion of surplus value production and realization. And it is this class relation that produces the increasingly lopsided distributions of wealth and power, along with the perpetual growth syndrome that exerts such enormous destructive pressure on global social relations and ecosystems.

How, then, can progressive forces organize to solve these problems, and how can the hitherto evasive dialectic between the dual imperatives of localized worker control and global coordinations be managed? It is in this context that I want to return to the foundational question of this inquiry: Can urban-based social movements play a constructive role and make their mark in the anti-capitalist struggle across these three dimensions? The answer depends in part upon some foundational reconceptualizations of the nature of class, and on the redefinition of the terrain of class struggles.

The conception of worker control that has hitherto dominated alternative left political thinking is problematic. The focus of struggle has been on the workshop and the factory as a privileged site of production of surplus value. The industrial working class has traditionally been privileged as the vanguard of the proletariat, its main revolutionary agent. But it was not factory workers who produced the Paris Commune. There is, for this reason, a dissident and influential view of the Commune that says it was not a proletarian uprising or a class-based movement at all, but an urban social movement that was reclaiming citizenship rights and the right to the city. It was not, therefore, anti-capitalist.[13]

I see no reason why it should not be construed as both a class struggle and a struggle for citizenship rights in the place where working people lived. To begin with, the dynamics of class exploitation are not confined to the workplace. Whole economies of dispossession and of predatory practices, of the sort described in Chapter 2 with respect to housing markets, are a case in point. These secondary forms of exploitation are primarily organized by merchants, landlords, and the financiers; and their effects are primarily felt in the living space, not in the factory. These forms of exploitation are and always have been vital to the overall dynamics of capital accumulation and the perpetuation of class power. Wage concessions to workers can, for example, be stolen back and recuperated for the capitalist class as a whole by merchant capitalists and landlords and, in contemporary conditions, even more viciously by the credit-mongers, the bankers, and the financiers. Practices of accumulation by dispossession, rental appropriations, by money- and profit-gouging, lie at the heart of many of the discontents that attach to the qualities of daily life for the mass of the population. Urban social movements typically mobilize around such questions, and they derive from the way in which the perpetuation of class power is organized around living as well as around working. Urban social movements therefore always have a class content even when they are primarily articulated in terms of rights, citizenship, and the travails of social reproduction.

The fact that these discontents relate to the commodity and monetary rather than the production circuit of capital matters not one wit: indeed, it is a big theoretical advantage to reconceptualize matters thus, because it focuses attention on those aspects of capital circulation that so frequently play the nemesis to attempts at worker control in production. Since it is capital circulation as a whole that matters (rather than merely what happens in the productive circuit), what does it matter to the capitalist class as a whole whether value is extracted from the commodity and money circuits rather than from the productive circuit directly? The gap between where surplus value is produced and where it is realized is as crucial theoretically as it is practically. Value created in production may be recaptured for the capitalist class from the workers by landlords charging high rents on housing.

Secondly, urbanization is itself produced. Thousands of workers are engaged in its production, and their work is productive of value and of surplus value. Why not focus, therefore, on the city rather than the factory as the prime site of surplus value production? The Paris Commune can then be reconceptualized as a struggle of that proletariat which produced the city to claim back the right to have and control that which they had produced. This is (and in the Paris Commune case was) a very different kind of proletariat to that which much of the left has typically cast in a vanguard role. It is characterized by insecurity, by episodic, temporary, and spatially diffuse employment, and is very difficult to organize on a workplace basis. But at this point in the history of those parts of the world characterized as advanced capitalism, the conventional factory proletariat has been radically diminished. So we now have a choice: mourn the passing of the possibility of revolution because that proletariat has disappeared, or change our conception of the proletariat to include the hordes of unorganized urbanization producers (of the sort that mobilized in the immigrant rights marches), and explore their distinctive revolutionary capacities and powers.

So who are these workers who produce the city? The city builders, the construction workers in particular, are the most obvious candidate even as they are not the only nor the largest labor force involved. As a political force, the construction workers have in recent times in the United States (and possibly elsewhere) all too often been supportive of the large-scale and class-biased developmentalism that keeps them employed. They do not have to be so. The masons and builders that Haussmann brought to Paris played an important role in the Commune. The "Green Ban" construction union movement in New South Wales in the early 1970s banned working on projects they deemed environmentally unsound, and were successful in much of what they did. They were ultimately destroyed by a combination of concerted state power and their own Maoist national leadership, who considered environmental issues a manifestation of flabby bourgeois sentimentality.[14]

But there is a seamless connection between those who mine the iron ore that goes into the steel that goes into the construction of the bridges across which the trucks carrying commodities travel to their final destinations of factories and homes for consumption. All of these activities (including spatial movement) are productive of value and of surplus value. If capitalism often recovers from crises, as we saw earlier, by "building houses and filling them with things," then clearly everyone engaged in that urbanizing activity has a central role to play in the macroeconomic dynamics of capital accumulation. And if maintenance, repairs, and replacements (often difficult to distinguish in practice) are all part of the value-producing stream (as Marx avers), then the vast army of workers involved in these activities in our cities is also contributing to value and surplus value production. In New York City thousands of workers are engaged in erecting scaffolding and taking it down again. They are producing value. If, furthermore, the flow of commodities from place of origin to final destination is productive of value, as Marx also insists, then so are the workers who are employed on the food chain that links rural producers to urban consumers. Thousands of delivery trucks clog the streets of New York City every day. Organized, those workers would have the power to strangle the metabolism of the city. Strikes of transport workers (as, for example, in France over the last twenty years, and now in Shanghai) are extremely effective political weapons (used negatively in Chile in the coup year of 1973). The Bus Riders Union in Los Angeles, and the organization of taxi drivers in New York and LA, are examples of organizing across these dimensions.[15] When the rebellious population of El Alto cut the main supply lines into La Paz, forcing the bourgeoisie to live on scraps, they soon gained their political objective. It is in fact in the cities that the wealthy classes are most vulnerable, not necessarily as persons but in terms of the value of the assets they control. It is for this reason that the capitalist state is gearing up for militarized urban struggles as the front line of class struggle in years to come.

Consider the flows not only of food and other consumer goods, but also of energy, water, and other necessities, and their vulnerabilities to disruption too. The production and reproduction of urban life, while some of it can be "dismissed" (an unfortunate word) as "unproductive" in the Marxist canon, is nevertheless socially necessary, part of the "faux frais" of the reproduction of the class relations between capital and labor. Much of this labor has always been temporary, insecure, itinerant, and precarious; and it very often fudges the supposed boundary between production and reproduction (as in the case of street vendors). New forms of organizing are absolutely essential for this labor force that produces and, just as importantly, reproduces the city. This is where newly fledged organizations come in, such as the Excluded Workers Congress in the

United Sates, which is an alliance of workers characterized by temporary and insecure conditions of employment, often, as with domestic workers, spatially scattered throughout a metropolitan region.[16]

The history of conventional labor struggles—and this is my third major point—also needs some rewriting. Most struggles waged by factory-based workers turn out, on inspection, to have had a much broader base. Margaret Kohn complains, for example, how left historians of labor laud the Turin Factory Councils of the early twentieth century while totally ignoring the "Houses of the People" in the community where much of the politics was shaped, and from which strong currents of logistical support flowed.[17] E. P. Thompson depicts how the making of the English working class depended as much upon what happened in chapels and in neighborhoods as in the workplace. The local city trades councils have played a much-underestimated role in British political organization, and often anchored the militant base of a nascent Labour Party and other left organizations in particular towns and cities in ways that the national union movement often ignored.[18] How successful would the Flint sit-down strike of 1937 have been in the United States had it not been for the masses of the unemployed and the neighborhood organizations outside the gates that unfailingly delivered their support, moral and material?

Organizing the neighborhoods has been just as important in prosecuting labor struggles, as has organizing the workplace. One of the strengths of the factory occupations in Argentina that followed on the collapse of 2001 is that the cooperatively managed factories also turned themselves into neighborhood cultural and educational centers. They built bridges between the community and the workplace. When past owners try to evict the workers or seize back the machinery, the whole populace typically turns out in solidarity with the workers to prevent such action.[19] When UNITE HERE sought to mobilize rank-and-file hotel workers around LAX airport in Los Angeles, they relied heavily "on extensive outreach to political, religious and other community allies, building a coalition" that could counter the employers' repressive strategies.[20] But there is, in this, also a cautionary tale: in the British miners' strikes of the 1970s and 1980s, the miners who lived in diffuse urbanized areas such as Nottingham were the first to cave in, while those in Northumbria, where workplace and living-place politics converged, maintained their solidarity to the end.[21] The problem posed by circumstances of this sort will be taken up later.

To the degree that conventional workplaces are disappearing in many parts of the so-called advanced capitalist world (though not, of course, in China or Bangladesh), organizing around not only work but also around conditions in the living space, while building bridges between the two, becomes even more crucial. But it has often been so in the past. Worker-controlled consumer cooperatives offered critical support during the Seattle general strike of 1919, and when the strike collapsed militancy shifted very markedly towards the development of an elaborate and interwoven system of mainly worker-controlled consumer cooperatives.[22]

As the lens is widened on the social milieu in which struggle is occurring, the sense of who the proletariat might be and what their aspirations and organizational strategies might be is transformed. The gender composition of oppositional politics looks very different when relations outside of the conventional factory (in both workplaces and living spaces) are brought firmly into the picture. The social dynamics of the workplace are not the same as those in the living space. On the latter terrain, distinctions based on gender, race, ethnicity, religion, and culture are frequently more deeply etched into the social fabric, while issues of social reproduction play a more prominent, even dominant role in the shaping of political subjectivities and consciousness. Conversely, the way capital differentiates and divides populations ethnically, racially, and across gender lines produces marked disparities in the economic dynamics of dispossession in the living space (thanks to the circuits of money and commodity capital). While the median loss of household wealth in the United States for everyone was 28 percent over the period 2005–09, that of Hispanics was 66 percent, and that of blacks 53 percent, while for whites it was 16 percent. The class character of ethnic discriminations in accumulation by dispossession, and the way these discriminations differentially affect neighborhood life, could not be plainer, particularly since most of the losses were due to falling housing values.[23] But it is also in neighborhood spaces that profound cultural ties based, for example, in ethnicity, religion, and cultural histories and collective memories can just as often bind as divide, to create the possibility of social and political solidarities in a completely different dimension to that which typically arises within the workplace.

There is a wonderful film that was produced by blacklisted Hollywood writers and directors (the so-called Hollywood Ten) in 1954 called *Salt of the Earth*. Based on actual events in 1951, it depicts the struggle of highly exploited Mexican-American workers and their families in a zinc mine in New Mexico. The Mexican workers demand equality with white workers, safer work conditions, and to be treated with dignity (a recurring theme in many anti-capitalist struggles). The women are distressed by the repeated failure of the male-dominated union to press home issues like sanitation and running water in the tied accommodations they inhabit. When the workers strike for their demands and are then banned from picketing under the Taft-Hartley Act provisions, the women take over the picket line (overcoming a lot of male opposition in the process). The men have to look after the children, only to learn the hard way how important running water and sanitation are to a reasonable daily life at home. Gender equality and feminist consciousness emerge as crucial weapons in the class struggle. When the sheriffs come to evict the families, popular support from other families (clearly based in cultural solidarities) not only sustains the striking families with food, but also puts them back into their tied housing. The company in the end has to cave in. The awesome power of unity between gender, ethnicity, working, and living is not easy to construct, and the tension in the film between men and women, between Anglo and Mexican workers, and between work-based and daily life perspectives, is just as significant as that between labor and capital. Only when unity and parity are constructed among all the forces of labor, the film says, will you be able to win. The danger this message represented for capital is measured by the fact that this is the only film ever to be systematically banned for political reasons from being shown in any US commercial venue for many years. Most of the actors were not professional; many were drawn from the miner's union. But the brilliant leading professional actress, Rosaura Revueltas, was deported to Mexico.[24]

In a recent book, Fletcher and Gapasin argue that the labor movement should pay more attention to geographical rather than sectoral forms of organization—that the US movement should empower the central labor councils in cities in addition to organizing sectorally.

> To the extent that labor speaks about matters of class, it should not see itself as separate from the community. The term *labor* should denote forms of organization with roots in the working class and with agendas that explicitly advance the class demands of the working class. In that sense, a community-based organization rooted in the working class (such as a worker's center) that addresses class-specific issues is a labor organization in the same way that a trade union is. To push the envelope a bit more, a trade union that addresses the interests of only one section of the working class (such as a white supremacist craft union) deserves the label *labor organization* less than does a community-based organization that assists the unemployed or the homeless.[25]

They therefore propose a new approach to labor organizing that

> essentially defies current trade union practices in forming alliances and taking political action. Indeed, it has the following central premise: *if class struggle is not restricted to the workplace, then neither should unions be.* The strategic conclusion is that unions must think in terms of organizing cities rather than simply organizing workplaces (or industries). And organizing cities is possible only if unions work with allies in metropolitan social blocks.[26]

"How then," they go on to ask "does one organize a city?" This, it seems to me, is one of the key questions that the left will have to answer if anti-capitalist struggle is to be revitalized in the years to come. Such struggles, as we have seen, have a distinguished history. The inspiration drawn from "Red Bologna" in the 1970s is a case in point. There has in fact been a long and distinguished history of "municipal socialism," and even whole phases of radical urban reform, such as that which occurred in "Red Vienna" or through the local radical municipal councils in Britain in the 1920s, which need to be recuperated as central to the history both of left reformism and of more revolutionary movements.[27] And it is one of those curious ironies of history that the French Communist Party distinguished itself far more in municipal administration (in part because it had no dogmatic theory or instructions from Moscow to guide it) than it did in other arenas of political life, from the 1960s even up to the present day. The British trade union councils likewise played a crucial role in urban politics, and rooted the militant power of local left parties. This tradition continued in the struggle by the municipalities in Britain against Thatcherism in the early 1980s. These were not only rearguard actions but, as in the case of the Greater London Council under Ken Livingstone in the early 1980s, potentially innovative, until Margaret Thatcher, recognizing the threat this urban-based opposition posed, abolished that whole layer of governance. Even in the United States, Milwaukee for many years had a socialist administration, and it is worth remarking that the only socialist ever elected to the US Senate began his career and earned the people's trust as mayor of Burlington, Vermont.

THE RIGHT TO THE CITY AS A POLITICAL CLASS-BASED DEMAND

If the participants in the Paris Commune were reclaiming their right to the city they had collectively helped produce, then why cannot "the right to the city" become a key mobilizing slogan for anti-capitalist struggle? The right to the city is, as was noted at the outset, an empty signifier full of immanent but not transcendent possibilities. This does not mean it is irrelevant or politically impotent; everything depends on who gets to fill the signifier with revolutionary as opposed to reformist immanent meaning.

It is not always easy to distinguish between reformist and revolutionary initiatives in urban settings. Participatory budgeting in Porto Alegre, ecologically sensitive programs in Curitiba, or living-wage campaigns in many US cities appear reformist (and rather marginal at that). The Chongqing initiative, described in Chapter 2, sounds on the surface more like an authoritarian version of Nordic paternalistic socialism rather than a revolutionary movement. But as their influence spreads, so initiatives of this sort reveal deeper layers of possibility for more radical conceptions and actions at the metropolitan scale. A spreading, revitalized rhetoric (originating in Brazil in the 1990s, but then moving from Zagreb to Hamburg to Los Angeles) over the right to the city, for example, seems to suggest something more revolutionary might be in prospect.[28] The measure of that possibility appears in the desperate attempts of existing political powers (for example, the NGOs and international institutions, including the World Bank, assembled at the Rio World Urban Forum in 2010) to co-opt that language to their own purposes.[29] In the same way that Marx depicted restrictions on the length of the working day as a first step down a revolutionary path, so claiming back the right for everyone to live in a decent house in a decent living environment can be seen as the first step towards a more comprehensive revolutionary movement.

There is no point in complaining at the attempt to co-opt. The left should take it as a compliment and battle to sustain its own distinctive immanent meaning: all those whose labors are engaged in producing and reproducing the city have a collective right not only to that which they produce, but also to decide what kind of urbanism is to be produced where, and how. Alternative democratic vehicles (other than the existing democracy of money power) such as popular assemblies need to be constructed if urban life is to be revitalized and reconstructed outside of dominant class relations.

The right to the city is not an exclusive individual right, but a focused collective right. It is inclusive not only of construction workers but also of all those who facilitate the reproduction of daily life: the caregivers and teachers, the sewer and subway repair men, the plumbers and electricians, the scaffold erectors and crane operators, the hospital workers and the truck, bus, and taxi drivers, the restaurant workers and the entertainers, the bank clerks and the city administrators. It seeks a unity from within an incredible diversity of fragmented social spaces and locations within innumerable divisions of labor. And there are many putative forms of organization—from workers' centers and regional workers' assemblies (such as that of Toronto) to alliances (such as the Right to the City alliances and the Excluded Workers Congress and other forms of organization of precarious labor) that have this objective upon their political radar.

But, for obvious reasons, it is a complicated right partly by virtue of the contemporary conditions of capitalist urbanization, as well as because of the nature of the populations that might actively pursue such a right. Murray Bookchin, for example, took the plausible view (also attributable to Lewis Mumford and many others influenced by the social anarchist tradition of thinking) that capitalist processes of urbanization have destroyed the city as a functioning body politic upon which a civilized anti-capitalist alternative might be built.[30] In a way, Lefebvre agrees, though in his case far more emphasis is placed on the rationalizations of urban space by state bureaucrats and technocrats to facilitate the reproduction of capital accumulation and of dominant class relations. The right to the contemporary suburb is hardly a viable anti-capitalist slogan.

It is for this reason that the right to the city has to be construed not as a right to that which already exists, but as a right to rebuild and re-create the city as a socialist body politic in a completely different image—one that eradicates poverty and social inequality, and one that heals the wounds of disastrous environmental degradation. For this to happen, the production of the destructive forms of urbanization that facilitate perpetual capital accumulation has to be stopped.

This was the sort of thing that Murray Bookchin argued for in pushing to create what he called a "municipal libertarianism" embedded in a bioregional conception of associated municipal assemblies rationally regulating their interchanges with each other, as well as with nature. It is at this point that the world of practical politics fruitfully intersects with the long history of largely anarchist-inspired utopian thinking and writing about the city.[31]

TOWARDS URBAN REVOLUTION

Three theses emerge from this history. First, work-based struggles, from strikes to factory takeovers, are far more likely to succeed when there is strong and vibrant support from popular forces assembled at the surrounding neighborhood or community level (including support from influential local leaders and their political organizations). This presumes that strong links between workers and local populations already exist or can be quickly constructed. Such links can arise "naturally" out of the simple fact that the workers' families constitute the community (as in the case of many mining communities of the sort portrayed in *Salt of the Earth*). But in more diffuse urban settings, there has to be a conscious political attempt to construct, maintain and strengthen such links. Where those links do not exist, as happened with the Nottinghamshire coal miners in the strikes of the 1980s in Britain, they have to be created. Otherwise such movements are far more likely to fail.

Secondly, the concept of work has to shift from a narrow definition attaching to industrial forms of labor to the far broader terrain of the work entailed in the production and reproduction of an increasingly urbanized daily life. Distinctions between work-based and community-based struggles start to fade away, as indeed does the idea that class and work are defined in a place of production in isolation from the site of social reproduction in the household.[32] Those who bring running water to our homes are just as important in the struggle for a better quality of life as those who make the pipes and the faucets in the factory. Those who deliver the food to the city (including the street vendors) are just as significant as those who grow it. Those who cook the food before it is eaten (the roasted-corn or hot-dog vendors on the streets, or those who slave away over the stoves in the household kitchens or over open fires) likewise add value to that food before it is digested. The collective labor involved in the production and reproduction of urban life must therefore become more tightly folded into left thinking and organizing. Earlier distinctions that made sense—between the urban and the rural, the city and the country—have in recent times also become moot. The chain of supply both into and out of the cities entails a continuous movement, and does not entail a break. Above all, the concepts of work and of class have to be fundamentally reformulated. The struggle for collective citizens' rights (such as those of immigrant workers) has to be seen as integral to anti-capitalist class struggle.

This revitalized conception of the proletariat embraces and includes the now massive informal sectors characterized by temporary, insecure, and unorganized labor. Groups in the population of this sort, it turns out, have historically played an important role in urban rebellions and revolts. Their action has not always been of a left character (but then neither can craft unions always claim that). They have often been susceptible to the blandishments of unstable or authoritarian charismatic leadership, secular or religious. For this reason the politics of such disorganized groups have often wrongly been dismissed by the conventional left as those of the "urban mob" (or, even more unfortunately, in Marxist lore as a "lumpenproletariat"), as much to be feared as embraced. It is imperative that these populations now be embraced as crucial to, rather than excluded from, anti-capitalist politics.

Finally, while the exploitation of living labor in production (in the broader sense already defined) must remain central to the conception of any anti-capitalist movement, struggles against the recuperation and realization of surplus value from workers in their living spaces have to be given equal status to struggles at the various points of production of the city. As in the case of temporary and insecure workers, the extension of class action in this direction poses organizational problems. But, as we shall see, it also holds out innumerable possibilities.

"HOW, THEN, DOES ONE ORGANIZE A CITY?"

The honest answer to Fletcher and Gapasin's question is: we simply do not know, partly because not enough hard thought has been given to the question, and partly because there is no systematic historical record of evolving political practices on which to base any generalizations. There have, of course, been brief periods of experimentation with "gas and water" socialist administration, or more adventurous urban utopianism, as in the Soviet Union in the 1920s.[33] But much of this easily faded into reformist socialist realism or paternalistic socialist/communist modernism (of which we see many touching relics in Eastern Europe). Most of what we now know about urban organization comes from conventional theories and studies of urban governance and administration within the context of bureaucratic capitalist governmentality (against which Lefebvre quite rightly endlessly railed), all of which is a far cry from the organization of an anti-capitalist politics. The best we have is a theory of the city as a corporate form, with all that this implies in terms of the possibilities of corporatist decision-making (which can, on occasion, when taken over by progressive forces, contest the more rabid forms of capitalist development and begin to address the questions of crippling and glaring social inequality and environmental degradations, at least at the local level, as happened in Porto Alegre and as was attempted in

Ken Livingstone's GLC). Alongside this, there is an extensive literature (usually in these times laudatory rather than critical) on the virtues of competitive urban entrepreneurialism, in which city administrations use a wide variety of incentives to attract (in other words, subsidize) investment.[34]

So how can we even begin to answer Fletcher and Gapasin's question? One way is to examine singular examples of urban political practices in revolutionary situations. So I close with a summary look at recent events in Bolivia, in the search for clues as to how urban rebellions might relate to anti-capitalist movements.

It was in the streets and squares of Cochabamba that a rebellion against neoliberal privatization was fought out in the famous "Water Wars" of 2000. Government policies were rebuffed, and two major international corporations—Bechtel and Suez—were forced out. And it was from El Alto, a teeming city on the plateau above La Paz, that rebellious movements arose to force the resignation of the pro-neoliberal president, Sánchez de Lozada, in October 2003, and to do the same to his successor, Carlos Mesa, in 2005. All of this paved the way for the national electoral victory of the progressive Evo Morales in December 2005. It was in Cochabamba also that an attempted counter-revolution by conservative elites against the presidency of Evo Morales was thwarted in 2007, as the conservative city administration fled the town in the face of the wrath of indigenous peoples who occupied it.

The difficulty, as always, is to understand the distinctive role local conditions played in these singular events, and to assess what universal principles (if any) we might derive from a study of them. This problem has bedeviled conflicting interpretations of the universal lessons that might be drawn from the Paris Commune of 1871. The advantage of a focus on contemporary El Alto, however, is that this is an ongoing struggle, and therefore open to continuous political interrogation and analysis. There already exist some excellent contemporary studies upon which to base interim conclusions.

Jeffrey Webber, for example, provides a compelling interpretation of events in Bolivia over the last decade or so.[35] He views the years 2000–05 as a genuinely revolutionary epoch in a situation of deep cleavage between elite and popular classes. Popular rejection of neoliberal policies with respect to the use of treasured natural resources on the part of a state ruled by a traditional elite (and backed by the forces of international capital) fused with a long-standing struggle for liberation from racial repression by an indigenous, largely peasant population. The violence of the neoliberal regime provoked uprisings that led to Morales's election in 2005. The entrenched elites (particularly concentrated in the city of Santa Cruz) subsequently launched a counter-revolutionary movement against the Morales government by demanding regional and local autonomy. This was an interesting move, because ideals of "local autonomy" have more often than not been embraced by the left in Latin America as central to its liberation struggles. It was often a demand of indigenous populations in Bolivia, and sympathetic academic theorists like Arturo Escobar tend to view such a demand as inherently progressive, if not a necessary precondition for anti-capitalist movements.[36] But the Bolivian case demonstrates that local or regional autonomy can be used by whatever party stands to benefit from shifting the locus of political and state decision-making to the particular scale that favors its own interests. This was what led Margaret Thatcher, for example, to abolish the Greater London Council, because it was a center of opposition to her policies. This is what animated Bolivian elites to seek the autonomy of Santa Cruz against the Morales government, which they saw as hostile to their interests. Having lost the national space, they sought to declare their local space autonomous.

While Morales' political strategy after his election has helped to consolidate the power of the indigenous movements, according to Webber he effectively abandoned the class-based revolutionary perspective that emerged in 2000–05 in favor of a negotiated and constitutional compromise with landed and capitalist elites (as well as accommodation to outside imperial pressures). The result, Webber argues, has been a "reconstituted neoliberalism" (with "Andean characteristics") after 2005, rather than any movement towards an anti-capitalist transition. The idea of a socialist transition has been postponed many years into the future. Morales has, however, taken a global leadership role on environmental issues by embracing the favored indigenous conception of "the rights of mother nature" in the Cochabamba declaration of 2010, and by incorporating this idea into the Bolivian constitution.

Webber's views have been vigorously contested, as might be expected, by supporters of the Morales regime.[37] I am not in a position to judge whether Morales' undoubtedly reformist and constitutional turn at the national level is a matter of political choice, expediency, or a necessity imposed by the configuration of class forces prevailing in Bolivia, backed by strong external imperialist pressures. Even Webber concedes that in the Cochabamba peasant-led uprising against a right-wing autonomist administration in 2007, it would have been disastrous adventurism for the radical initiative to go against the constitutionalism of the Morales government by permanently replacing the elected conservative government officials who had fled the city by a popular assembly form of government.[38]

What role has urban organization played in these struggles? This is an obvious question, given the key roles of Cochabamba and El Alto as centers of repeated rebellions and the role of Santa Cruz as the center of the counter-revolutionary movement. In Webber's account, El Alto, Cochabamba, and Santa Cruz all appear as mere sites where the forces of class opposition and populist indigenous movements happened to play out. He does at one point note, however, that "the 80-percent-indigenous, informal proletarian city of El Alto—with its rich insurrectionary traditions of revolutionary Marxism from 'relocated' ex-miners, and indigenous radicalism from the Aymara, Quechua, and other indigenous rural-to-urban migrants—played the most important role at the height of sometimes bloody confrontations with the state." He also notes that

the rebellions, in their best moments, were characterized by assembly-style, democratic, and mass-based mobilization from below, drawing upon the organizational patterns of the Trotskyists and anarcho-syndicalist tin miners—the vanguard of the Bolivian left for much of the twentieth century—and variations of the indigenous *ayllus*—traditional communitarian structures—adapted to new rural and urban contexts.[39]

But we know little more than this from Webber's account. The particular conditions pertaining at the different sites of struggle are largely ignored (even when he provides a blow-by-blow account of the 2007 rebellion in Cochabamba) in favor of an account of the class and populist forces in motion within Bolivia in general, against the background of external imperialist pressures. It is therefore interesting to turn to the studies of the anthropologists Leslie Gill and Sian Lazar, both of whom provide in-depth portrayals of conditions, social relations, and putative organizational forms prevailing in El Alto at different historical moments. Gill's study, *Teetering on the Rim*, published in 2000, detailed conditions prevailing in the 1990s, while Lazar's study, *El Alto, Rebel City*, published in 2010, was based on field work in El Alto both before and after the rebellion of 2003.[40] Neither Gill nor Lazar anticipated the possibility of rebellion before it happened. While Gill recorded plenty of politics occurring on the ground in the 1990s, the movements were so fragmented and confused (particularly given the negative role of the NGOs that had displaced the state as the main providers of social services) as to seem to preclude any coherent mass movement, even though the schoolteachers' strike that occurred during her field-work was fiercely fought out in explicitly class-conscious terms. Lazar was also taken by surprise by the rebellion of October 2003, and returned to El Alto after it occurred to try to reconstruct the circumstances that had given rise to it.

El Alto is a special kind of place, and it is important to lay out the particularities.[41] It is a relatively new city (only incorporated in 1988) of immigrants on the inhospitable Altiplano, high up above La Paz, largely populated by rural peasants driven off the land—by the gradual commercialization of agricultural production; by displaced industrial workers (particularly those from the tin mines that had been rationalized, privatized, and in some instances closed down from the mid 1980s onwards); and by low-income refugees from La Paz, where high land and housing costs had for some years been pushing poorer people to look for living space elsewhere. There was not, therefore, a strongly entrenched bourgeoisie in El Alto, as there was in La Paz and Santa Cruz. It was, as Gill puts it, a city "where many victims of Bolivia's ongoing experiment with free-market reform teeter on the edge of survival." The steady withdrawal of the state, from the mid 1980s, from administration and service-provision under neoliberal privatization meant that local state controls were relatively weak. Populations had to hustle and self-organize to survive, or rely on the dubious help of NGOs supplemented by donations and favors extracted from political parties in return for support at election times. But three of the four main supply routes into La Paz pass through El Alto, and the power to choke them off became important in the struggles that occurred. The urban-rural continuum (with the rural dominated largely by indigenous peasant populations with distinctive cultural traditions and forms of social organization, like the *ayllus* that Webber mentions) was an important feature to the metabolism of the city. The city mediated between the urbanity of La Paz and the rurality of the region, both geographically and ethno-culturally. Flows of people and of goods throughout the region circulated around and through El Alto, while the daily commute from El Alto into La Paz rendered the latter city dependent on El Alto for much of its low-wage labor force.

Older forms of collective organization of labor in Bolivia had been disrupted in the 1980s with the closure of the tin mines, but had earlier constituted "one of the most militant working classes in Latin America."[42] The miners had played a key role in the revolution of 1952, which led to the nationalization of the tin mines, and had likewise led the way in bringing down the repressive Hugo Banzer regime in 1978. Many of the displaced miners ended up in El Alto after 1985 and, by Gill's account, experienced great difficulty in adjusting to their new situation. But it would later become clear that their political class consciousness, animated by Trotskyism and anarcho-syndicalism, did not entirely disappear. It was to become an important resource (though how important is a matter of dispute) in subsequent struggles, beginning with the 1995 teachers' strike that Gill studied in detail. But their politics shifted in important ways. With no choice "but to participate in the poorly paid and insecure work that engaged the vast majority of El Alto's residents," the miners went from a situation in which the class enemy and their own solidarity was clear, to one in which they had to answer a different and far more difficult strategic question: "[H]ow can they construct a form of solidarity in El Alto from an ethnically diverse social constituency characterized by widely different individual histories, a mosaic of work relations, and intense internal competitiveness?"[43]

This transition, forced upon the miners through neoliberalization, is by no means unique to Bolivia or El Alto. It poses the same dilemma that hits displaced steel workers in Sheffield, Pittsburgh, and Baltimore. In fact it is a pretty universal dilemma wherever the vast wave of deindustrialization and privatization unleashed since the mid 1970s or so has hit home. How it was confronted in Bolivia is therefore of more than passing interest.

"New kinds of trade union structures have emerged," writes Lazar,

> especially those of the peasants and the informal sector workers in the cities … They are based upon coalitions of smallholders, even micro-capitalists, who do not work for one boss in one place, where they can be easily targeted by the army. Their household model of production allows for fluidity of associational life, but has also allowed them to form alliances and organizations based upon territorial location; the street where they sell, the village or region where they live and farm, and, with the addition of the *vecino* organizational structures in the cities, their zone.

In this, the association between people and places becomes extremely important as the source of common bonds. While these bonds can just as often be agonistic as harmonious, the face-to-face contacts are frequent and therefore incipiently strong.

> Trade unions are flourishing in the informal economy of El Alto and form a crucial part of the structure of civic organization that is parallel to the state and that shapes multi-tiered citizenship in the city. They do so in a context where economic competition between individuals is painfully exaggerated and where one would therefore expect political collaboration to be difficult if not downright impossible.

While the social movements often fall prey to severe factionalism and infighting, they "are beginning to build a more coherent ideology out of the particularity of the different sectoral demands."[44] The residual collective class consciousness and organizational experience of the displaced tin miners thereby became a critical resource. When coupled with practices of local democracy resting on indigenous traditions of local and popular decision-making assemblies (the *ayllus*), the subjective conditions for creating alternative political associations were partially realized. As a result, "the working class in Bolivia is reconstituting itself as a political subject, *albeit not in its traditional form*."[45]

Hardt and Negri also take up this point in their own appropriation of the Bolivian struggle in support of their theory of multitude.

All relations of hegemony and representation within the working class are thus thrown into question. It is not even possible for the traditional unions to represent adequately the complex multiplicity of class subjects and experiences. This shift, however, signals no farewell to the working class or even a decline of worker struggle but rather an increasing multiplicity of the proletariat and a new physiognomy of struggles.[46]

Lazar partially concurs with this theoretical reformulation, but provides much more fine-grained detail on how the working-class movement comes to be constituted. As she sees it, "the nested affiliation of an alliance of associations, each one with local forms of accountability, is one of the sources of the social movements' strength in Bolivia." These organizations were often hierarchical, and sometimes authoritarian rather than democratic. But "if we view democracy as the will of the people, the corporatist side of Bolivian politics makes sense as one of its most important democratic (albeit not necessarily egalitarian) traditions." The anticapitalist victories of the sort that saw off major corporate enemies such as Bechtel and Suez "would not have been possible without the mundane experiences of collective democracy that are part of alteños' day-to-day lives."[47]

Democracy is organized in El Alto, according to Lazar, along three distinctive lines. The neighborhood associations are place-bound organizations that exist not only to provide collective local goods but also to mediate the many conflicts that arise between residents. The overarching Association of Neighborhood Associations largely exists as a forum for resolving conflicts between neighborhoods. This is a classic "nested hierarchical" form, but one in which all sorts of mechanisms exist, which Lazar examines in detail, to ensure that leaders either rotate or stay faithful to their base (a principle which, until the Tea Party came along, would be anathema in US politics).

The second pinion comprises the sectoral associations of various groups in the population, such as street vendors, transport workers, and the like. And again, much of the work of these associations is devoted to mediating conflicts (for example, between individual street vendors). But it is in this way that precarious workers in the so-called informal sector are organized (a lesson to be learned by the "Excluded Workers" movement in the United States). This form of organization possesses tentacles reaching far back down the supply chain of, for example, fish and food-stuffs from the surrounding areas. Through these links it is capable of easily and instantaneously mobilizing the insurrectionary capacities of surrounding peasant and rural populations—or, conversely, of organizing immediate responses in the city to rural massacres and repressions. These geographical ties were strong, and overlapped with those of the neighborhood associations to which many peasant migrant families belonged, while maintaining links back to their villages of origin.

Thirdly, there were more conventional unions, the most important of which was that of the schoolteachers who, ever since the strike of 1995, had been in the forefront of militancy (as was also the case in Oaxaca in Mexico). The trade unions had a local, regional, and national organizational structure that continued to function in negotiations with the state, even though they had been much weakened by the neoliberal assault upon regular employment and traditional forms of trade union organization over the preceding thirty years.

But there is something else at work in El Alto that Lazar is at great pains to integrate into her account. Underlying values and ideals are particularly strong, and are often upheld and articulated through popular cultural events and activities—fiestas, religious festivals, dance events—as well as through more direct forms of collective participation, such as the popular assemblies (in the neighborhoods and within the formal and informal trade unions). These cultural solidarities and collective memories enable unions to overcome tensions "and promote a collective sense of self, which in turn enables them to be effective political subjects."[48] The greatest of these tensions is that between leadership and the base. Both place-based and sectoral forms of organization exhibit similar characteristics, in which popular bases "attempt to assert collective values in the face of leaders' perceived individualism." The mechanisms are complex, but in Lazar's account there seem to be multiple informal means by which issues of collectivism and individualism, solidarity and factionalism, are worked out. Furthermore, the "trade union" and the "communitarian" forms of organization are not distinct traditions, but frequently fuse culturally through the "syncretic appropriation of political traditions, drawing on trade unionisms, populism, and indigenous democratic values and practices. It is the creative mixing of these different

threads that has enabled El Alto to overcome its political marginalization at the national level and take center stage."[49] These were the sorts
of bonds "that coalesce at particular moments, such as Cochabamba in
2000, the peasant blockades of the altiplano of April and September 2000,
February and October of 2003 in El Alto and La Paz and January–March
2005 in El Alto."

El Alto has become such an important focus for this new politics,
Lazar maintains, largely because of the ways in which the sense of citizenship has been constituted in the city. This is an important issue because it
presages the possibility of class and indigenous rebellion being organized
through solidarities based in common citizenship. Historically, of course,
this has always been a central feature of the French revolutionary tradition. In El Alto this sense of belonging and solidarity is

> constituted as a mediated relationship between citizen and state that is
> shaped by the structure of collective civic organization parallel to the state
> at zone, citywide and national levels. In 1999, the political party ... lost
> its hold over these organizations and over the city in general, enabling
> a more oppositional stance to emerge; this coincided with the fact that
> alteños have been radicalized by increasing economic hardship. The pro-
> tests of September and October 2003 and subsequent years derive their
> strength from the domination of these particular political circumstances
> with much more long-standing processes of identification with the
> countryside and the construction of a collective sense of self.

Lazar goes on to conclude that

> citizenship in the indigenous city of El Alto involves a mix of urban and
> rural, collectivism and individualism, egalitarianism and hierarchy. The
> alternative visions of democracy that are being produced have reinvig-
> orated national and regional indigenous movements by the ways that
> they combine class-based and nationalist concerns with identity poli-
> tics, through the contestation over the ownership of the means of social
> reproduction and the nature of the state.

The two communities that were most salient for her in all of this "are
based on residence at zonal and city levels, and on occupation at the city
level."[50] It is through the idea of citizenship that agonistic relations in

both the workplace and the living space are converted into a powerful form of social solidarity.

These diverse social processes (which Lazar is at pains not to romanticize in ways that so much of the academic left does) had a singular effect on how the city itself came to be regarded. "It is pertinent to ask," she writes,

> what is it that makes El Alto a city rather than a slum, a suburb, a marketplace, or a transport hub. My answer is that different actors, in both the state system and in nonstate places, are in the process of making a distinctive and separate identity for El Alto. That identity is of course not singular, but is becoming increasingly bound up with political radicalism and indigeneity.

And it was "the conversion of that identity and its emergent political consciousness into political action" in 2003 and 2005 that brought El Alto to not only national but international attention as a "rebel city."[51]

The lesson to be learned from Lazar's account is that it is indeed possible to build a political city out of the debilitating processes of neoliberal urbanization, and thereby reclaim the city for anti-capitalist struggle. While the events of October 2003 should be understood as "a highly contingent coming together of different sectoral interests that exploded into something much more when the government ordered the army to kill the demonstrators," the preceding years of organizing those sectoral interests and the building of a sense of the city as "a center of radicalism and indigeneity" cannot be ignored.[52] The organization of informal laborers along traditional union lines, the pulling together of the Federation of neighborhood associations, the politicization of urban-rural relations, the creation of nested hierarchies and of leadership structures alongside egalitarian assemblies, the mobilization of the forces of culture and of collective memories—all provide models for thinking about what might consciously be done to reclaim cities for anti-capitalist struggle. The forms of organization that came together in El Alto in fact bear a strong resemblance to some of the forms that came together in the Paris Commune (the arrondissements, the unions, the political factions, and the strong sense of citizenship in and loyalty to the city).

FUTURE MOVES

While, in the case of El Alto, all of this can be seen as an outcome of contingent circumstances that just happened to come together, why cannot we imagine consciously building a city-wide anti-capitalist movement along such lines? Imagine in New York City, for example, the revival of the now largely somnolent community boards as neighborhood assemblies with budget-allocation powers, along with a merged Right to the City Alliance and Excluded Workers Congress agitating for greater equality in incomes and access to health care and housing provision, all coupled with a revitalized local Labor Council to try to rebuild the city and the sense of citizenship and social and environmental justice out of the wreckage being wrought by neoliberal corporatist urbanization. What the story of El Alto suggests is that such a coalition will work only if the forces of culture and of a politically radical tradition (which most certainly exists in New York, as it also does in Chicago, San Francisco, and Los Angeles) can be mobilized in such a way as to animate citizen-subjects (however fractious, as indeed is always the case in New York) behind a radically different project of urbanization to that dominated by the class interests of developers and financiers determined to "build like Robert Moses with Jane Jacobs in mind."

But there is one hugely important jester in this otherwise rosy-looking scenario for the development of anti-capitalist struggle. For what the Bolivian case also demonstrates, if Webber is only half right, is that any anti-capitalist drive mobilized through successive urban rebellions has to be consolidated at some point at a far higher scale of generality, lest it all lapse back at the state level into parliamentary and constitutional reformism that can do little more than reconstitute neoliberalism within the interstices of continuing imperial domination. This poses more general questions not only of the state and state institutional arrangements of law, policing, and administration, but of the state system within which all states are embedded. Much of the contemporary left, unfortunately, is reluctant to pose these questions even as it struggles from time to time to come up with some form of macro-organization, such as Murray Bookchin's radical "confederalism" or Elinor Ostrom's mildly reformist "polycentric governance," which looks suspiciously like a state system, sounds like a state system, and will almost surely act like a state system no matter what the intent of its proponents might be.[53] It is either that, or lapse into the kind of incoherence that has Hardt and Negri in *Commonwealth* smash the state on page 361 only to resurrect it on page 380 as the guarantor of a universal minimum standard of living, as well as of universal health care and education.[54]

But it is precisely here that the question of how one organizes a whole city becomes so crucial. It liberates progressive forces from being organizationally locked into the micro-level of struggling worker collectives and solidarity economies (important those these may be), and forces upon us a completely different way of both theorizing and practicing an anti-capitalist politics. From a critical perspective it is possible to see precisely why Ostrom's preference for "polycentric government" must fail, along with Bookchin's "confederal" municipal libertarianism. "If the whole society were to be organized as a confederation of autonomous municipalities," writes Iris Young, "then what would prevent the development of large-scale inequality and injustice among communities [of the sort described in Chapter 3] and thereby the oppression of individuals who do not live in the more privileged and more powerful communities?"[55] The only way to avoid such outcomes is for some higher authority both to mandate and enforce those cross-municipality transfers that would roughly equalize at least opportunities, and perhaps outcomes as well. This is what Murray Bookchin's confederal system of autonomous municipalities would almost certainly be unable to achieve, to the degree that this level of governance is barred from making policy and firmly restricted to the administration and governance of things, and effectively barred from the governance of people. The only way that general rules of, say, redistribution of wealth between municipalities can be established is either by democratic consensus (which, we know from historical experience, is unlikely to be voluntarily and informally arrived at) or by citizens as democratic subjects with powers of decision at different levels within a structure of hierarchical governance. To be sure, there is no reason why all power should flow downwards in such a hierarchy, and mechanisms can surely be devised to prevent dictatorship or authoritarianism. But the plain fact is that certain problems of, for example, the common wealth, only become visible at particular scales, and it is only appropriate that democratic decisions be made at those scales.

From this standpoint the movement in Bolivia might want to look southwards for inspiration, at how the movement initially concentrated in Santiago in Chile has morphed from students demanding from the state free and egalitarian educational provision into an anti-neoliberal alliance of movements demanding of the state constitutional reform, improved pension provision, new labor laws, and a progressive personal and corporate tax system to begin to reverse the slide into ever greater social inequality in Chilean civil society. The question of the state, and in particular what kind of state (or non-capitalist equivalent), cannot be avoided even in the midst of immense contemporary skepticism, on both the left and the right of the political spectrum, of the viability or desirability of such a form of institutionalization.

The world of citizenship and rights, within some body-politic of a higher order, is not necessarily opposed to that of class and struggle. Citizen and comrade can march together in anti-capitalist struggle, albeit often working at different scales. But this can occur only if we become, as Park long ago urged, more "conscious of the nature of our task," which is collectively to build the socialist city on the ruins of destructive capitalist urbanization. That is the city air that can make people truly free. But this entails a revolution in anti-capitalist thinking and practices. Progressive anti-capitalist forces can more easily mobilize to leap forward into global coordinations via urban networks that may be hierarchical but not monocentric, corporatist but nevertheless democratic, egalitarian and horizontal, systemically nested and federated (imagine a league of socialist cities much as the Hanseatic League of old became the network that nourished the powers of merchant capitalism), internally discordant and contested, but solidarious against capitalist class power—and, above all, deeply engaged in the struggle to undermine and eventually overthrow the power of the capitalist laws of value on the world market to dictate the social relations under which we work and live. Such a movement must open the way for universal human flourishing beyond the constraints of class domination and commodified market determinations. The world of true freedom begins, as Marx insisted, only when such material constraints are left behind. Reclaiming and organizing cities for anti-capitalist struggles is a great place to begin.

CHAPTER SIX

London 2011: Feral Capitalism Hits the Streets

" Nihilistic and feral teenagers," the *Daily Mail* called them: the crazy youths from all walks of life who raced around the streets of London desperately and often mindlessly hurling bricks, stones, and bottles at the cops, while looting here and setting bonfires there, leading the authorities on a merry chase of catch-as-catch-can as they tweeted their way from one strategic target to another.

The word "feral" pulled me up short. It reminded me of how the communards in Paris in 1871 were depicted as wild animals, as hyenas, that deserved to be (and often were) summarily executed in the name of the sanctity of private property, morality, religion, and the family. But the word conjured up another association: Tony Blair attacking the "feral media," having for so long been comfortably lodged in the left pocket of Rupert Murdoch, only later to be substituted as Murdoch reached into his right pocket to pluck out David Cameron.

There will of course be the usual hysterical debate between those prone to view the riots as a matter of pure, unbridled, and inexcusable criminality, and those anxious to contextualize events against a background of bad policing, continuing racism and unjustified persecution of youths and minorities, mass unemployment of the young, burgeoning social deprivation, and a mindless politics of austerity that has nothing to do with economics and everything to do with the perpetuation and consolidation of personal wealth and power. Some may even get around to condemning the meaningless and alienating qualities of so many jobs and so much of daily life in the midst of immense but unevenly distributed potentiality for human flourishing.

If we are lucky, we will have commissions and reports to say all over again what was said of Brixton and Toxteth in the Thatcher years. I say "lucky" because the feral instincts of the current British prime minister seem more attuned to turning on water cannons, to calling in the tear gas brigade, and using rubber bullets, while pontificating unctuously about the loss of moral compass, the decline of civility, and the sad deterioration of family values and discipline among errant youths.

But the problem is that we live in a society where capitalism itself has become rampantly feral. Feral politicians cheat on their expenses; feral bankers plunder the public purse for all it's worth; CEOs, hedge fund operators, and private equity geniuses loot the world of wealth; telephone and credit card companies load mysterious charges on everyone's bills; corporations and the wealthy don't pay taxes while they feed at the trough of public finance; shopkeepers price-gouge; and, at the drop of a hat swindlers and scam artists get to practice three-card monte right up into the highest echelons of the corporate and political world.

A political economy of mass dispossession, of predatory practices to the point of daylight robbery—particularly of the poor and the vulnerable, the unsophisticated and the legally unprotected—has become the order of the day. Does anyone believe it is possible to find an honest capitalist, an honest banker, an honest politician, an honest shopkeeper, or an honest police commissioner anymore? Yes, they do exist. But only as a minority that everyone else regards as stupid. Get smart. Get easy profits. Defraud and steal! The odds of getting caught are low. And in any case there are plenty of ways to shield personal wealth from the costs of corporate malfeasance.

What I say may sound shocking. Most of us don't see it because we don't want to. Certainly no politician dare say it, and the press would only print it to heap scorn upon the sayer. But my guess is that every street rioter knows exactly what I mean. They are only doing what everyone else is doing, though in a different way—more blatantly and visibly, in the streets. They mimic on the streets of London what corporate capital is doing to planet earth. Thatcherism unchained the inherently feral instincts of capitalism (the "animal spirits" of the entrepreneur, apologists coyly named them), and nothing has transpired to curb them since. Reckless slash-and-burn is now openly the motto of the ruling classes pretty much everywhere.

This is the new normal in which we live. This is what the next grand commission of inquiry should address. Everyone, not just the rioters, should be held to account. Feral capitalism should be put on trial for crimes against humanity, as well as for crimes against nature.

Sadly, this is what the mindless rioters cannot see or demand. Everything conspires to prevent us from seeing and demanding it also. This is why political power so hastily dons the robes of superior morality and unctuous reason, so that no one might see it as so nakedly corrupt and stupidly irrational.

But there are various glimmers of hope and light around the world. The *indignados* movements in Spain and Greece, the revolutionary impulses in Latin America, the peasant movements in Asia, are all beginning to see through the vast scam that a predatory and feral global capitalism has unleashed upon the world. What will it take for the rest of us to see and act upon it? How can we begin all over again? What direction should we take? The answers are not easy. But one thing we do know for certain: we can only get to the right answers by asking the right questions.

CHAPTER SEVEN

#OWS: The Party of Wall Street Meets Its Nemesis

The Party of Wall Street has ruled unchallenged in the United States for far too long. It has totally dominated the policies of presidents over at least four decades, if not longer, no matter whether individual presidents have been its willing agents or not. It has legally corrupted Congress via the craven dependency of politicians in both political parties upon its raw money power and upon access to the mainstream media that it controls. Thanks to the appointments made and approved by presidents and Congress, the Party of Wall Street dominates much of the state apparatus as well as the judiciary—in particular the Supreme Court, whose partisan judgments increasingly favor venal money interests, in spheres as diverse as electoral, labor, environmental, and contract law.

The Party of Wall Street has one universal principle of rule: that there shall be no serious challenge to the absolute power of money to rule absolutely. That power must be exercised with one objective: those possessed of money power shall not only be privileged to accumulate wealth endlessly at will, but they shall have the right to inherit the earth, not only taking either direct or indirect dominion of the land and all the resources and productive capacities that reside therein, but also assuming absolute command, directly or indirectly, over the labor and creative potentialities of all those others it needs. The rest of humanity shall be deemed disposable.

These principles and practices do not arise out of individual greed, short-sightedness, or mere malfeasance (although all of these are plentifully to be found). These principles have been carved into the body politic of our world through the collective will of a capitalist class animated by the coercive laws of competition. If my lobbying group spends less than yours, then I will get less in the way of favors. If a jurisdiction spends on people's needs, it shall be deemed uncompetitive.

Many decent people are locked into the embrace of a system that is rotten to the core. If they are to earn even a reasonable living they have no other job option except to give the devil his due: they are only "following orders," as Eichmann famously claimed, "doing what the system demands," as others now put it, in acceding to the barbarous and immoral principles and practices of the Party of Wall Street. The coercive laws of competition force us all, to some degree, to obey the rules of this ruthless and uncaring system. The problem is systemic, not individual.

The party's favored slogans of freedom and liberty to be guaranteed by private property rights, free markets, and free trade actually translate into the freedom to exploit the labor of others, to dispossess the assets of the common people at will, and to pillage the environment for individual or class benefit.

Once in control of the state apparatus, the Party of Wall Street typically privatizes all the juicy morsels at less than market value to open new terrains for their capital accumulation. They arrange subcontracting (the military-industrial complex being a prime example) and taxation practices (subsidies to agri-business and low capital gains taxes) that permit them freely to ransack the public coffers. They deliberately foster such complicated regulatory systems and such astonishing administrative incompetence within the rest of the state apparatus (remember the EPA under Reagan, and FEMA and "heck-of-a-job" Brown under Bush) as to convince an inherently skeptical public that the state can never play a constructive or supportive role in improving the daily life or the future prospects of anyone. And, finally, they use the monopoly of violence that all sovereign states claim to exclude the public from much of what passes for public space and to harass, put under surveillance, and if necessary criminalize and incarcerate all those who do not broadly accede to their dictates. They excel in practices of repressive tolerance that perpetuate the illusion of freedom of expression, as long as that expression does not ruthlessly expose the true nature of their project and the repressive apparatus upon which it rests.

The Party of Wall Street ceaselessly wages class war. "Of course there is class war," says Warren Buffett, "and it is my class, the rich, who are making it and we are winning." Much of this war is waged in secret, behind a series of masks and obfuscations through which the aims and objectives of the Party of Wall Street are disguised.

The Party of Wall Street knows all too well that, when profound political and economic questions are transformed into cultural issues, they become unanswerable. It regularly calls up a huge range of captive expert opinion, for the most part employed in the think tanks and universities they fund and splattered throughout the media they control, to create controversies out of all manner of issues that simply do not matter, and to propose solutions to questions that do not exist. One minute they talk of nothing other than the austerity necessary for everyone else to cure the deficit, and the next they are proposing to reduce their own taxation no matter what impact this may have on the deficit. The one thing that can never be openly debated and discussed is the true nature of the class war they have been so ceaselessly and ruthlessly waging. To depict something as "class war" is, in the current political climate and in their expert judgment, to place it beyond the pale of serious consideration—even to be branded a fool, if not seditious.

But now, for the first time, there is an explicit movement to confront the Party of Wall Street and its unalloyed money power. The "street" in Wall Street is being occupied—oh horror upon horrors—by others! Spreading from city to city, the tactics of Occupy Wall Street are to take a central public space, a park or a square, close to where many of the levers of power are centered, and, by putting human bodies in that place, to convert public space into a political commons—a place for open discussion and debate over what that power is doing and how best to oppose its reach. This tactic, most conspicuously re-animated in the noble and ongoing struggles centered on Tahrir Square in Cairo, has spread across the world (Puerta del Sol in Madrid, Syntagma Square in Athens, and now the steps of St Paul's Cathedral in London and Wall Street itself). It shows us that the collective power of bodies in public space is still the most effective instrument of opposition when all other means of access are blocked. What Tahrir Square showed to the world was an obvious truth: that it is bodies on the street and in the squares, not the babble of sentiments on Twitter or Facebook, that really matter.

The aim of this movement in the United States is simple. It says: "We the people are determined to take back our country from the moneyed powers that currently run it. Our aim is to prove Warren Buffett wrong. His class, the rich, shall no longer rule unchallenged nor automatically inherit the earth. Nor is his class, the rich, always destined to win." It says: "We are the 99 percent. We have the majority and this majority can, must and shall prevail. Since all other channels of expression are closed to us by money power, we have no other option except to occupy the parks, squares and streets of our cities until our opinions are heard and our needs attended to."

To succeed, the movement has to reach out to the 99 percent. This it can do and is doing, step by step. First there are all those being plunged into immiseration by unemployment, and all those who have been or are now being dispossessed of their houses and their assets by the Wall Street phalanx. The movement must forge broad coalitions between students, immigrants, the underemployed, and all those threatened by the totally unnecessary and draconian austerity politics being inflicted upon the nation and the world at the behest of the Party of Wall Street. It must focus on the astonishing levels of exploitation in workplaces—from the immigrant domestic workers who the rich so ruthlessly exploit in their homes to the restaurant workers who slave for almost nothing in the kitchens of the establishments in which the rich so grandly eat. It must bring together the creative workers and artists whose talents are so often turned into commercial products under the control of big-money power.

The movement must above all reach out to all the alienated, the dissatisfied, and the discontented—all those who recognize and feel in their gut that there is something profoundly wrong, that the system the Party of Wall Street has devised is not only barbaric, unethical, and morally wrong, but also broken.

All this has to be democratically assembled into a coherent opposition, which must also freely contemplate the future outlines of an alternative city, an alternative political system, and, ultimately, an alternative way of organizing production, distribution, and consumption for the benefit of the people. Otherwise, a future for the young that points to spiraling private indebtedness and deepening public austerity, all for the benefit of the 1 percent, is no future at all.

In response to the Occupy Wall Street movement, the state, backed by capitalist class power, makes an astonishing claim: that they and only they have the exclusive right to regulate and dispose of public space. The public has no common right to public space! By what right do mayors, police chiefs, military officers, and state officials tell us, the people, that they have the right to determine what is public about "our" public space and who may occupy that space when? When did they presume to evict us, the people, from any space we decide collectively and peacefully to occupy? They claim they are taking action in the public interest (and cite laws to prove it), but it is we who are the public! Where is "our interest" in all of this? And, by the way, is it not "our" money that the banks and financiers so blatantly use to accumulate "their" bonuses?

In the face of the organized power of the Party of Wall Street to divide and rule, the movement that is emerging must also take as one of its founding principles that it will be neither divided nor diverted until the Party of Wall Street is brought either to its senses—to see that the common good must prevail over narrow venal interests—or to its knees. Corporate privileges that confer the rights of individuals without the responsibilities of true citizens must be rolled back. Public goods such as education and health care must be publicly provided and made freely available. The monopoly powers in the media must be broken. The buying of elections must be ruled unconstitutional. The privatization of knowledge and culture must be prohibited. The freedom to exploit and dispossess others must be severely curbed, and ultimately outlawed.

Americans believe in equality. Polling data show they believe (no matter what their general political allegiances might be) that the top 20 percent of the population might be justified in claiming 30 percent of the total wealth, but that they now control 85 percent of it is unacceptable. That most of that wealth is controlled by the top 1 percent is totally unacceptable. What the Occupy Wall Street movement proposes is that we, the people of the United States, commit to a reversal of that level of inequality—not only in terms of wealth and income, but even more importantly, in terms of the political power that such a disparity confers and reproduces. The people of the United States are rightly proud of their democracy, but it has always been endangered by capital's corruptive power. Now that it is dominated by that power the time is surely nigh, as Jefferson long ago suggested would be necessary, to make another American revolution: one based on social justice, equality, and a caring and thoughtful approach to the relation to nature.

The struggle that has broken out—that of the People versus the Party of Wall Street—is crucial to our collective future. The struggle is global as well as local in nature. It brings together students who are locked in a life-and-death struggle with political power in Chile to create a free and quality education system for all, and so begin the dismantling of the neoliberal model that Pinochet so brutally imposed. It embraces the agitators in Tahrir Square, who recognize that the fall of Mubarak (like the end of Pinochet's dictatorship) was but the first step in an emancipatory struggle to break free from money power. It includes the *indignados* in Spain, the striking workers in Greece, the militant opposition emerging all around the world, from London to Durban, Buenos Aires, Shenzhen, and Mumbai. The brutal dominions of big capital and sheer money power are everywhere on the defensive.

Whose side will each of us, as individuals, come down on? Which street will we occupy? Only time will tell. But what we do know is that the time is now. The system is not only broken and exposed, but incapable of any response other than repression. So we, the people, have no option but to struggle for the collective right to decide how that system shall be reconstructed, and in whose image. The Party of Wall Street has had its day, and has failed miserably. The construction of an alternative on its ruins is both an opportunity and an inescapable obligation that none of us can or would ever want to avoid.

Acknowledgments

I would like to thank the editors of the publications listed below for permission to use material that appeared previously under their auspices.

Chapter 1 is a slightly modified version of an article published in *New Left Review* 53, September–October 2008 entitled "The Right to the City."

Chapter 2 is a slightly expanded version of the first part of an article published in *Socialist Register 2011* entitled "The Urban Roots of Financial Crises: Reclaiming the City for Anti-Capitalist Struggle."

Chapter 3 is based on a piece entitled "The Future of the Commons," published in *Radical History Review* 109 (2011). I thank Charlotte Hess for pointing out some serious omissions in the original article with respect to the work of Elinor Ostrom, and the participants in a seminar organized under the auspices of 16 Beaver in New York City, whose discussions on the topic of the commons helped greatly in clarifying my own ideas.

Chapter 4 is a slightly modified version of an article entitled "The Art of Rent: Globalization, Monopoly and Cultural Production," first published in *Socialist Register 2002*.

Chapter 5 is an extended version of the last part of an article first published in *Socialist Register 2011* entitled "The Urban Roots of Financial Crises: Reclaiming the City for Anti-Capitalist Struggle."

I would like to thank the participants in the "Right to the City" reading group in New York City (Peter Marcuse in particular) along with the members of the seminar in the Center for Place, Culture and Politics in the City University of New York for the many stimulating discussions over the last few years.

Notes

PREFACE: HENRI LEFEBVRE'S VISION

1. Henri Lefebvre, *La Proclamation de la Commune*, Paris: Gallimard, 1965; *Le Droit à la Ville*, Paris: Anthropos, 1968; *L'Irruption, de Nanterre au Sommet*, Paris: Anthropos, 1968; *La Révolution Urbaine*, Paris: Gallimard, 1970; *Espace et Politique (Le Droit à la Ville, II)*, Paris: Anthropos, 1973; *La Production de l'Espace*, Paris: Anthropos, 1974.
2. James Holston, *Insurgent Citizenship*, Princeton: Princeton University Press, 2008.
3. Ana Sugranyes and Charlotte Mathivet, eds, *Cities for All: Proposals and Experiences Towards the Right to the City*, Santiago, Chile: Habitat International Coalition, 2010; Neil Brenner, Peter Marcuse and Margit Mayer, eds, *Cities for People, and Not for Profit: Critical Urban Theory and the Right to the City*, New York: Routledge, 2011.

CHAPTER ONE: THE RIGHT TO THE CITY

1. Robert Park, *On Social Control and Collective Behavior*, Chicago: Chicago University Press, 1967: 3.
2. Friedrich Engels, *The Condition of the Working-Class in England in 1844*, London: Penguin Classics, 2009; Georg Simmel, "The Metropolis and Mental Life," in David Levine, ed., *On Individualism and Social Forms*, Chicago: Chicago University Press, 1971.

3. Mike Davis, *Planet of Slums*, London: Verso, 2006.

4. For a fuller account of these ideas see David Harvey, *The Enigma of Capital, and The Crises of Capitalism*, London: Profile Books, 2010.

5. This account is based on David Harvey, *Paris, Capital of Modernity*, New York: Routledge, 2003.

6. Robert Moses, "What Happened to Haussmann," *Architectural Forum* 77 (July 1942): 57–66; Robert Caro, *The Power Broker: Robert Moses and the Fall of New York*, New York: Knopf, 1974.

7. Henri Lefebvre, *The Urban Revolution*, Minneapolis: University of Minnesota Press, 2003.

8. William Tabb, *The Long Default: New York City and the Urban Fiscal Crisis*, New Cork: Monthly Review Press, 1982; David Harvey, *A Brief History of Neoliberalism*, Oxford: OUP, 2005.

9. Thomas Campanella, *The Concrete Dragon: China's Urban Revolution and What it Means for the World*, Princeton, NJ: Princeton Architectural Press, 2008.

10. Richard Bookstaber, *A Demon of Our Own Design: Markets, Hedge Funds, and the Perils of Financial Innovation*, New York: Wiley, 2007; Frank Partnoy, *Infectious Greed: How Deceit and Risk Corrupted Financial Markets*, New York: Henry Holt, 2003.

11. Harvey, *A Brief History of Neoliberalism*; Thomas Edsall, *The New Politics of Inequality*, New York: Norton, 1985.

12. Jim Yardley and Vikas Bajaj, "Billionaires' Ascent Helps India, and Vice Versa," *New York Times*, July 27, 2011.

13. Marcello Balbo, "Urban Planning and the Fragmented City of Developing Countries," *Third World Planning Review* 15: 1 (1993): 23–5.

14. Friedrich Engels, *The Housing Question*, New York: International Publishers (1935): 74–7.

15. Marshall Berman, *All That Is Solid Melts Into Air*, London: Penguin, 1988.

16. Friedrich Engels, *The Housing Question*: 23.

17. Usha Ramanathan "Illegality and the Urban Poor," *Economic and Political Weekly*, July 22, 2006; Rakesh Shukla, "Rights of the Poor: An Overview of Supreme Court," *Economic and Political Weekly*, September 2, 2006.

18. Much of this thinking follows the work of Hernando de Soto, *The Mystery of Capital: Why Capitalism Triumphs in the West and Fails Everywhere Else*, New York: Basic Books, 2000; see the critical examination by Timothy Mitchell, "The Work of Economics: How a Discipline Makes its World," *Archives Européennes de Sociologie* 46: 2 (2005): 297–320.

19. Julia Elyachar, *Markets of Dispossession: NGOs, Economic Development, and the State in Cairo*, Chapel Hill, NC: Duke University Press, 2005.

20. Ananya Roy, *Poverty Capital: Microfinance and the Making of Development*, New York: Routledge, 2010; C.K. Prahalad, *The Fortune at the Bottom of the Pyramid: Eradicating Poverty Through Profits*, New York: Pearson Prentice Hall, 2009.

21. Scott Larson, "Building Like Moses with Jane Jacobs in Mind," PhD dissertation, Earth and Environmental Sciences Program, City University of New York, 2010.

CHAPTER TWO: THE URBAN ROOTS OF CAPITALIST CRISES

1. Robert Shiller, "Housing Bubbles are Few and Far Between," *New York Times*, February 5, 2011.

2. "It is indeed shocking," writes Charles Leung, in "Macroeconomics and Housing: A Review of the Literature," *Journal of Housing Economics* 13 (2004): 249–67, "that there has been so little overlap and interaction between the macroeconomics and the housing literature."

3. *World Development Report 2009: Reshaping Economic Geography*, Washington, DC: World Bank, 2009; David Harvey, "Assessment: Reshaping Economic Geography: The World Development Report," *Development and Change Forum 2009*, 40: 6 (2009): 1,269–78.

4. *World Development Report*: 206. Three of the authors of the report subsequently responded to criticisms from geographers, but avoided any consideration of the foundational criticisms I raised (such as that "land is not a commodity," and that there is an unexamined relation between macroeconomic crises and housing and urbanization policies), on the astonishing grounds that all I was really claiming was "that the recent sub-prime mortgage crisis in the USA implies that housing finance has no role to play in addressing shelter needs of the poor in developing countries," and that this was, in their opinion, "outside the realm of the report." They therefore totally ignored the main thrust of my criticism. See Uwe Deichmann, Indermit Gill and Chor-Ching Goh, "Texture and Tractability: The Framework for Spatial Policy Analysis in the *World Development Report 2009*," *Cambridge Journal of Regions, Economy and Society* 4: 2 (2011): 163–74. The one group of economists who have long seen the significance of how "real estate values and construction have peaked shortly before major depressions" and "played a major role in creating the boom and the subsequent

bust" are followers of Henry George, but unfortunately they are also totally ignored by mainstream economists. See Fred Foldvary, "Real Estate and Business Cycles: Henry George's Theory of the Trade Cycle," paper presented at the Lafayette College Henry George Conference, June 13, 1991.

5. Graham Turner, *The Credit Crunch: Housing Bubbles, Globalisation and the Worldwide Economic Crisis*, London: Pluto, 2008; David Harvey, *The Condition of Postmodernity*, Oxford: Basil Blackwell, 1989: 145–6, 169.

6. Cf. David Harvey, *The New Imperialism*, Oxford: OUP, 2003: 113, where I pointed out that some 20 percent of GDP growth in the United States in 2002 was attributable to mortgage refinancing, and that even at that time the "potential bursting of the property bubble" was therefore "a matter of serious concern."

7. William Tabb, *The Long Default: New York City and the Urban Fiscal Crisis*, New York: Monthly Review Press, 1982; David Harvey, *A Brief History of Neoliberalism*, Oxford: OUP, 2005; Ashok Bardhan and Richard Walker, "California, Pivot of the Great Recession," UC Berkeley, CA: Institute for Research on Labor and Employment, 2010.

8. William Goetzmann and Frank Newman, "Securitization in the 1920s," *Working Papers*, National Bureau of Economic Research, 2010; Eugene White, "Lessons from the Great American Real Estate Boom and Bust of the 1920s," *Working Papers*, National Bureau of Economic Research, 2010; Kenneth Snowden, "The Anatomy of a Residential Mortgage Crisis: A Look Back to the 1930s," *Working Papers*, National Bureau of Economic Research, 2010. A central conclusion they all draw is that greater awareness of what then happened would surely have helped policy-makers avoid the chronic mistakes of recent times—an observation that the World Bank economists might want to take to heart. In a paper published in 1940—"Residual, Differential and Absolute Urban Ground Rents and Their Cyclical Fluctuations," *Econometrica* 8 (1940): 62–78—Karl Pribam showed how "construction in Great Britain and Germany anticipated business contraction or expansion by one to three years" in the period before World War I.

9. See the measured evaluations and contributions of Brett Christophers: "On Voodoo Economics: Theorising Relations of Property, Value and Contemporary Capitalism," *Transactions, Institute of British Geographers*, New Series, 35 (2010): 94–108; "Revisiting the Urbanization of Capital," *Annals of the Association of American Geographers* 101 (2011): 1–18.

10. Karl Marx, *Grundrisse*, London: Penguin, 1973: 88–100.

11. For more details, see David Harvey, "History versus Theory: A Commentary on Marx's Method in *Capital*," forthcoming in *Historical Materialism*.
12. Karl Marx, *Capital*, Volume 2, London: Penguin, 1978: 357. My emphasis.
13. Marx, *Grundrisse*: 89.
14. Mario Tronti, "The Strategy of Refusal," Turin: Einaudi, 1966, English translation at Libcom.org; Antonio Negri, *Marx Beyond Marx: Lessons on the Grundrisse*, London: Autonomedia, 1989.
15. Karl Marx, *Capital*, Volume 3, London: Penguin, Chapters 24 and 25.
16. David Harvey, *The Limits to Capital*, Oxford: Blackwell, 1982, Chapter 8.
17. Marx, *Capital*, Volume 3: 597; Geoffrey Harcourt, *Some Cambridge Controversies in the Theory of Capital*, Cambridge: CUP, 1972. My emphasis.
18. Marx, *Capital*, Volume 3: 573. Both Isaac and Émile, incidentally, were part of the utopian Saint-Simonian movement prior to 1848.
19. David Harvey, *The Urbanisation of Capital*, Oxford: Blackwell, 1985; and *The Enigma of Capital, And the Crises of Capitalism*, London: Profile Books, 2010; Brett Christophers, "Revisiting the Urbanization of Capital," *Annals of the Association of American Geographers* 101: 6 (2011): 1–11.
20. Brinley Thomas, *Migration and Economic Growth: A Study of Great Britain and the Atlantic Economy*, Cambridge: CUP, 1973.
21. Leo Grebler, David Blank, and Louis Winnick, *Capital Formation in Residential Real Estate*, Princeton, NJ: Princeton University Press, 1956.
22. The devastating and unseemly details of all this are spelled out in Gretchen Morgenson and Joshua Rosner, *Reckless Endangerment: How Outsized Ambition, Greed and Corruption Led to Economic Armageddon*, New York: Times Books, 2011.
23. Marx, *Capital*, Volume 3, Chapter 25.
24. Marx, *Capital*, Volume 1, London: Penguin, 1973: 793 similarly notes how capital can manipulate both the demand for and supply of surplus labor through, for example, investment and technologically induced unemployment.
25. Michael Lewis, *The Big Short: Inside the Doomsday Machine*, New York: Norton, 2010: 34.
26. Marx, *Capital*, Volume 3: 597.
27. John Logan and Harvey Molotch, *Urban Fortunes: The Political Economy of Place*, Berkeley, CA: University of California Press, 1987.
28. Lewis, *The Big Short*: 141.
29. Lewis, *The Big Short*: 93.
30. See entry "Cities in the Great Depression," wikipedia.org.
31. Martin Boddy, *The Building Societies*, London: Macmillan, 1980.
32. Binyamin Appelbaum, "A Recovery that Repeats Its Painful Precedents," *New York Times Business Section*, July 28, 2011.

33. The Kerner Commission, *Report of the National Advisory Commission on Civil Disorders*, Washington, DC: Government Printing Office, 1968.

34. Appelbaum, "A Recovery that Repeats Its Painful Precedents."

35. Jonathan Weisman, "Reagan Policies Gave Green Light to Red Ink," *Washington Post*, June 9, 2004: A11; William Greider, "The Education of David Stockman," *Atlantic Monthly*, December 1981.

36. Warren Buffett, interviewed by Ben Stein, "In Class Warfare, Guess Which Class Is Winning," *New York Times*, November 26, 2006; David Stockman, "The Bipartisan March to Fiscal Madness," *New York Times*, April 23, 2011.

37. Karl Marx and Friedrich Engels, *The Communist Manifesto*, London: Pluto Press, 2008: 4.

38. Barbara Ehrenreich and Dedrich Muhammad, "The Recession's Racial Divide," *New York Times*, September 12, 2009.

39. Morgenson and Rosner, *Reckless Endangerment*.

40. Kevin Chiu, "Illegal Foreclosures Charged in Investigation," *Housing Predictor*, April 24, 2011.

41. Lynne Sagalyn, "Mortgage Lending in Older Neighborhoods," *Annals of the American Academy of Political and Social Science* 465 (January 1983): 98–108; Manuel Aalbers, ed., *Subprime Cities: The Political Economy of Mortgage Markets*, New York: John Wiley, 2011.

42. Annette Bernhardt, Ruth Milkman, Nik Theodore, Douglas Heckathorn, Michael Auer, James DeFillippis, Ana Gonzalez, Victor Narro, Jason Perelshteyn, Diana Polson, and Michael Spiller, *Broken Laws, Unprotected Workers: Violations of Employment and Labor Laws in America's Cities*, New York: National Employment Law Project, 2009.

43. Keith Bradsher, "China Announces New Bailout of Big Banks," *New York Times*, January 7, 2004.

44. For a general overview, see Thomas Campanella, *The Concrete Dragon: China's Urban Revolution and What it Means for the World*, Princeton, NJ: Princeton Architectural Press, 2008. I also tried to assemble a general picture of China's urbanization in Chapter 5 of *A Brief History of Neoliberalism*.

45. David Barboza, "Inflation in China Poses Big Threat to Global Trade," *New York Times*, April 17, 2011; Jamil Anderlini, "Fate of Real Estate Is Global Concern," *Financial Times*, June 1, 2011; Robert Cookson, "China Bulls Reined in by Fears on Economy," *Financial Times*, June 1, 2011.

46. Keith Bradsher, "China's Economy is Starting to Slow, but Threat of Inflation Looms," *New York Times*, Business Section, May 31, 2011.

47. Wang Xiaotian, "Local Governments at Risk of Defaulting on Debt," *China Daily*, June 28, 2011; David Barboza, "China's Cities Piling Up Debt to Fuel Boom," *New York Times*, July 7, 2011.

48. David Barboza, "A City Born of China's Boom, Still Unpeopled," *New York Times*, October 20, 2010.
49. Jamil Anderlini, "Fate of Real Estate is Global Concern," *Financial Times*, June 1, 2011.
50. International Monetary Fund/International Labour Organization, *The Challenges of Growth, Employment and Social Cohesion*, Geneva: International Labour Organization, 2010.
51. Keith Bradsher, "High-Speed Rail Poised to Alter China, but Costs and Fares Draw Criticism," *New York Times*, June 23, 2011.
52. Peter Martin and David Cohen, "Socialism 3.0 in China," the-diplomat. com; Anderlini, "Fate of Real Estate is Global Concern."

CHAPTER THREE: THE CREATION OF THE URBAN COMMONS

1. Garrett Hardin, "The Tragedy of the Commons," *Science* 162 (1968): 1,243–8; B. McCay and J. Acheson, eds, *The Question of the Commons: The Culture and Ecology of Communal Resources*, Tucson, AZ: University of Arizona Press, 1987.
2. It is astonishing how many left analysts get Hardin totally wrong on this point. Thus, Massimo de Angelis, *The Beginning of History: Value Struggles and Global Capital*, London: Pluto Press, 2007: 134, writes that "Hardin has engineered a justification for privatization of the commons space rooted in an alleged natural necessity."
3. Elinor Ostrom, *Governing the Commons: The Evolution of Institutions for Collective Action*, Cambridge: CUP, 1990.
4. Eric Sheppard and Robert McMaster, eds, *Scale and Geographic Inquiry*, Oxford: Blackwell, 2004.
5. One anarchist theorist who does take this problem seriously is Murray Bookchin, in *Remaking Society: Pathways to a Green Future*, Boston, MA: South End Press, 1990; and *Urbanization without Cities: The Rise and Decline of Citizenship*, Montreal: Black Rose Books, 1992. Marina Sitrin, *Horizontalism: Voices of Popular Power in Argentina*, Oakland, CA: AK Press, 2006, provides a stirring defense of anti-hierarchical thinking. See also Sara Motta and Alf Gunvald Nilson, *Social Movements in the Global South: Dispossession, Development and Resistance*, Basingstoke, Hants: Palgrave Macmillan, 2011. A leading theorist of this hegemonic anti-hierarchical view on the left is John Holloway, *Change the World without Taking Power*, London: Pluto Press, 2002.

6. Jacques Rancière, cited in Michael Hardt and Antonio Negri, *Common-wealth*, Cambridge, MA: Harvard University Press, 2009: 350.

7. Elizabeth Blackmar, "Appropriating 'the Common': The Tragedy of Property Rights Discourse," in Setha Low and Neil Smith, eds, *The Politics of Public Space*, New York: Routledge, 2006.

8. Margaret Kohn, *Radical Space: Building the House of the People*, Ithaca, NY: Cornell University Press, 2003.

9. Charlotte Hess and Elinor Ostrom, *Understanding Knowledge as a Commons: From Theory to Practice*, Cambridge, MA: MIT Press, 2006.

10. Hardt and Negri, *Commonwealth*: 137–9.

11. Martin Melosi, *The Sanitary City: Urban Infrastructure in America, from Colonial Times to the Present*, Baltimore, MD: Johns Hopkins, 1999.

12. Anthony Vidler, "The Scenes of the Street: Transformations in Ideal and Reality, 1750–1871," in Stanford Anderson, *On Streets: Streets as Elements of Urban Structure*, Cambridge, MA: MIT Press, 1978.

13. *World Development Report 2009: Reshaping Economic Geography*, Washington, DC: World Bank, 2009; Ananya Roy, *Poverty Capital: Microfinance and the Making of Development*, New York: Routledge, 2010.

14. Ronald Meek, *Studies in the Labour Theory of Value*, New York: Monthly Review Press, 1989.

15. Ellen Meiksins Wood, *Empire of Capital*, London: Verso, 2005.

16. Karl Marx, *Capital*, Volume 1, New York: Vintage, 1977: 169–70.

17. Ibid., 171.

18. Ibid., 714.

19. Robin Blackburn, "Rudolph Meidner, 1914–2005: A Visionary Pragmatist," *Counterpunch*, December 22, 2005.

20. Hardt and Negri have recently revived general interest in this important idea (*Commonwealth*: 258).

21. United Workers Organization and National Economic and Social Rights Initiative, *Hidden in Plain Sight: Workers at Baltimore's Inner Harbor and the Struggle for Fair Development*, Baltimore and New York, 2011; Sian Lazar, *El Alto, Rebel City: Self and Citizenship in Andean Bolivia*, Durham, NC: Duke University Press, 2010.

22. Karl Marx, *Capital*, Volume 1: 638.

23. David Harvey, *The Enigma of Capital, And the Crises of Capitalism*, London: Profile Books, 2010.

24. Elinor Ostrom, "Beyond Markets and States: Polycentric Governance of Complex Economic Systems," *American Economic Review* 100 (3): 200, 641–72.

25. Elinor Ostrom, "Polycentric Approach for Coping with Climate Change,"

Background Paper to the 2010 World Development Report, Washington, DC: World Bank, Policy Research Working Paper 5095, 2009.

26. Andrew Sancton, *The Assault on Local Government*, Montreal: McGill-Queen's University Press, 2000: 167 (cited in Ostrom, "Polycentric Approach for Coping with Climate Change").

27. Vincent Ostrom, "Polycentricity—Part 1," in Michael McGinnis, ed, *Polycentricity and Local Public Economies*, Ann Arbor, MI: University of Michigan Press, 1999 (cited in Ostrom, "Polycentric Approach for Coping with Climate Change").

28. Charles Tiebout, "A Pure Theory of Local Expenditures," *Journal of Political Economy* 64: 5 (1956): 416–24.

29. Murray Bookchin, *Urbanization Without Cities: The Rise and Decline of Citizenship*, Montreal: Black Rose Books, 1992: Chapters 8 and 9.

30. Silvia Federici, "Women, Land Struggles and the Reconstruction of the Commons," *Working USA: The Journal of Labor and Society* 14 (2011): 41–56.

CHAPTER FOUR: THE ART OF RENT

1. Daniel Bell, *The Cultural Contradictions of Capitalism*, New York: Basic Books, 1978: 20; David Harvey, *The Condition of Postmodernity*, Oxford: Basil Blackwell, 1989: 290–1, 347–9; Brandon Taylor, *Modernism, Postmodernism, Realism: A Critical Perspective for Art*, Winchester: Winchester School of Art Press, 1987: 77.

2. The general theory of rent to which I am appealing is presented in David Harvey, *The Limits to Capital*, Oxford: Basil Blackwell, 1982: Chapter 11.

3. Karl Marx, *Capital*, Volume 3, New York: International Publishers, 1967: 774–5.

4. Cited in Douglas Kelbaugh, *Common Place*, Seattle: University of Washington Press, 1997: 51.

5. Wolfgang Haug, "Commodity Aesthetics," Working Papers Series, Department of Comparative American Cultures, Washington State University, 2000: 13.

6. Marx's views on monopoly rent are summarized in Harvey, *The Limits to Capital*: Chapter 5.

7. Alfred Chandler, *The Visible Hand: The Managerial Revolution in American Business*, Cambridge, MA: Harvard University Press, 1977.

8. Marx, *Capital*, Volume 3: 246. See also Harvey, *The Limits to Capital*: Chapter 5.

9. Karl Marx, *Grundrisse*, Harmondsworth: Penguin, 1973: 524–39. For a general expansion of this argument, see Harvey, *The Limits to Capital*: Chapter 12; and David Harvey, *The Condition of Postmodernity*, Part 3; and for a specific application of the concept see William Cronon, *Nature's Metropolis*, New York: Norton, 1991.

10. Tahbilk Wine Club, *Wine Club Circular* 15 (June 2000), Tahbilk Winery and Vineyard, Tahbilk, Victoria, Australia.

11. William Langewiesche, "The Million Dollar Nose," *Atlantic Monthly* 286: 6 (December 2000): 11–22.

12. Bob Jessop, "An Entrepreneurial City in Action: Hong Kong's Emerging Strategies in Preparation for (Inter-)Urban Competition," *Urban Studies* 37: 12 (2000): 2,287–313; David Harvey, "From Managerialism to Entrepreneurialism: The Transformation of Urban Governance in Late Capitalism," *Geografiska Annaler* 71B (1989): 3–17; Neil Brenner, *Spaces of Neoliberalism: Urban Restucturing in North America and Western Europe*, Oxford: Wiley-Blackwell, 2003.

13. See Kevin Cox, ed, *Spaces of Globalization: Reasserting the Power of the Local*, New York: Guilford Press, 1997.

14. John Logan and Harvey Molotch, *Urban Fortunes: The Political Economy of Place*, Berkeley: University of California Press, 1988.

15. Pierre Bourdieu, *Distinction: A Social Critique of the Judgement of Taste*, London: Routledge & Kegan Paul, 1984.

16. Miriam Greenberg, *Branding New York: How a City in Crisis Was Sold to the World*, New York: Routledge, 2008.

17. Donald McNeill, *Urban Change and the European Left: Tales from the New Barcelona*, New York: Routledge, 1999.

18. Argyro Loukaki, "Whose Genius Loci: Contrasting Interpretations of the Sacred Rock of the Athenian Acropolis," *Annals of the Association of American Geographers* 87: 2 (1997): 306–29.

19. Rebecca Abers, "Practicing Radical Democracy: Lessons from Brazil," *Plurimondi* 1: 2 (1999): 67–82; Ignacio Ramonet, "Porto Alegre," *Le Monde Diplomatique* 562: 1 (January 2001).

CHAPTER FIVE: RECLAIMING THE CITY FOR ANTI-CAPITALIST STRUGGLE

1. The saying "city air makes one free" comes from medieval times, when incorporated towns with charters could function as "non-feudal islands in a feudal sea." The classic account is Henri Pirenne, *Medieval Cities*, Princeton, NJ: Princeton University Press, 1925.

2. Stephen Graham, *Cities Under Siege: The New Military Urbanism*, London: Verso, 2010.

3. Kevin Jonson and Hill Ong Hing, "The Immigrants Rights Marches of 2006 and the Prospects for a New Civil Rights Movement," *Harvard Civil Rights-Civil Liberties Law Review* 42: 99–138.

4. Thomas Mertes, ed, *A Movement of Movements*, London: Verso, 2004; Sara Motta and Alf Gunvald Nilson, eds, *Social Movements in the Global South: Dispossession, Development and Resistance*, Basingstoke, Hants: Palgrave Macmillan, 2011.

5. Karl Marx and Vladimir Lenin, *The Civil War in France: The Paris Commune*, New York: International Publishers, 1989.

6. Mario Tronti, "Workers and Capital," at libcom.org, first published in Italian, 1971.

7. Immanuel Ness and Dario Azzelini, eds, *Ours to Master and to Own: Workers' Control from the Commune to the Present*, London: Haymarket Books, 2011.

8. Karl Marx, *Capital*, Volume 2, London: Penguin, 1978; David Harvey, *A Companion to Marx's Capital, Volume 2*, London: Verso, forthcoming.

9. David Harvey, *A Brief History of Neoliberalism*, Oxford: OUP, 2005.

10. Murray Bookchin, *Urbanization Without Cities: The Rise and Decline of Citizenship*, Montreal: Black Rose Books, 1992.

11. David Graeber, *Direct Action: An Ethnography*, Oakland, CA: AK Press, 2009: 239. See also Ana Dinerstein, Andre Spicer, and Steffen Bohm, "The (Im)possibilities of Autonomy, Social Movement in and Beyond Capital, the State and Development," *Non-Governmental Public Action Program, Working Papers*, London School of Economics and Political Science, 2009.

12. Mondragon is one of the most instructive cases of worker self-management that has stood the test of time. Founded under fascism in 1956 as a worker-cooperative in the Basque Country of Spain, it now has some 200 enterprises throughout Spain and into Europe. In most cases the difference in remuneration among the shareholders is limited to 3:1, compared to around 400:1 in most US corporations (though in some instances in recent years the ratios within Mondragon have risen to 9:1). The corporate enterprise operates across all three circuits of capital by setting up credit institutions and retail outlets in addition to production units. This may be one of the reasons it has survived. Left critics complain at the lack of solidarity with labor struggles more generally, and point to some of its exploitative corporatist sub-contracting practices and the internal efficiency measures needed to keep the corporation competitive. But if all capitalist enterprises were of this sort, we would be living in a very

different world. It cannot easily be dismissed. George Cheney, *Values at Work: Employee Participation Meets Market Pressure at Mondragon*, Ithaca, NY: ILR Press, 1999.

13. Manuel Castells, *The City and the Grassroots*, Berkeley, CA: University of California Press, 1983; Roger Gould, *Insurgent Identities: Class, Community, and Protest in Paris from 1848 to the Commune*, Chicago: University of Chicago Press, 1995. For my rebuttal of these arguments, see David Harvey, *Paris, Capital of Modernity*, New York: Routledge, 2003.

14. John Tully, "Green Bans and the BLF: The Labour Movement and Urban Ecology," *International Viewpoint* IV 357 (March 2004).

15. Michael Wines, "Shanghai Truckers' Protest Ebbs with Concessions Won on Fees," *New York Times*, April 23, 2011; Jacqueline Levitt and Gary Blasi, "The Los Angeles Taxi Workers Alliance," in Ruth Milkman, Joshua Bloom, and Victor Narro, eds, *Working for Justice: The LA Model of Organizing and Advocacy*, Ithaca, NY: Cornell University Press, 2010: 109–24.

16. Excluded Workers Congress, *Unity for Dignity: Excluded Workers Report*, New York, Excluded Workers Congress, c/o Inter-Alliance Dialogue, December 2010.

17. Margaret Kohn, *Radical Space: Building the House of the People*, Ithaca, NY: Cornell University Press, 2003.

18. Edward Thompson, *The Making of the English Working Class*, Harmondsworth, Middlesex: Penguin Books, 1968.

19. Peter Ranis, "Argentina's Worker-Occupied Factories and Enterprises," *Socialism and Democracy* 19: 3 (November 2005): 1–23; Carlos Forment, "Argentina's Recuperated Factory Movement and Citizenship: An Arendtian Perspective," Buenos Aires: Centro de Investigación de la Vida Publica, 2009; Marcela López Levy, *We Are Millions: Neo-liberalism and New Forms of Political Action in Argentina*, London: Latin America Bureau, 2004.

20. Forrest Stuart, "From the Shop to the Streets: UNITE HERE Organizing in Los Angeles Hotels," in Ruth Milkman, Joshua Bloom, and Victor Narro, eds, *Working for Justice: The LA Model of Organizing and Advocacy*, Ithaca, NY: Cornell University Press, 2010.

21. Huw Beynon, *Digging Deeper: Issues in the Miner's Strike*, London: Verso, 1985.

22. Dana Frank, *Purchasing Power: Consumer Organizing, Gender, and the Seattle Labor Movements, 1919–29*, Cambridge: CUP, 1994.

23. Peter Whoriskey, "Wealth Gap Widens between Whites, Minorities, Report Says," *Washington Post*, Business Section, July 26, 2011.

24. James Lorence, *The Suppression of Salt of the Earth: How Hollywood, Big Labor and Politicians Blacklisted a Movie in Cold War America*, Albuquerque:

University of New Mexico Press, 1999. The film can be downloaded for free.

25. Bill Fletcher and Fernando Gapasin, *Solidarity Divided: The Crisis in Organized Labor and a New Path Toward Social Justice*, Berkeley, CA: University of California Press, 2008: 174.

26. Ibid.

27. Max Jäggi, *Red Bologna*, Littlehampton: Littlehampton Book Services, 1977; Helmut Gruber, *Red Vienna: Experiment in Working-Class Culture, 1919–34*, Oxford: OUP, 1991.

28. Rebecca Abers, *Inventing Local Democracy: Grassroots Politics in Brazil*, Boulder, CO: Lynne Reinner Publisher, 2000. On the living wage movement, see Robert Pollin, Mark Brenner, and Jeanette Wicks-Lim, *A Measure of Fairness: The Economics of Living Wages and Minimum Wages in the United States*, Ithaca, NY: Cornell University Press, 2008. For a particular case, see David Harvey, *Spaces of Hope*, Edinburgh: Edinburgh University Press, 2000; Ana Sugranyes and Charlotte Mathivet, eds, *Cities for All: Proposals and Experiences Towards the Right to the City*, Santiago, Chile: Habitat International Coalition, 2010.

29. Peter Marcuse, "Two World Forums, Two Worlds Apart," at www. plannersnetwork.org.

30. Murray Bookchin, *The Limits of the City*, Montreal: Black Rose Books, 1986.

31. The history of this trend begins with Patrick Geddes, *Cities in Evolution*, Oxford: Oxford University Press (first published in 1915), and passes mainly through the influential figure of Lewis Mumford, in his *The City in History: Its Origins, Its Transformations, and Its Prospects*, Orlando, FL: Harcourt, 1968.

32. Ray Pahl, *Divisions of Labour*, Oxford: Basil Blackwell, 1984.

33. Anatole Kopp, *Ville et Révolution*, Paris: Editions Anthropos, 1967.

34. Gerald Frug, *City Making: Building Communities without Building Walls*, Princeton, NJ: Princeton University Press, 1999; Neil Brenner and Nik Theodore, *Spaces of Neoliberalism: Urban Restructuring in North America and Western Europe*, Oxford: Wiley Blackwell, 2003.

35. Jeffrey Webber, *From Rebellion to Reform in Bolivia: Class Struggle, Indigenous Liberation, and the Politics of Evo Morales*, Chicago: Haymarket Books, 2011. Several Spanish-language sources are cited in Michael Hardt and Antonio Negri, *Commonwealth*, Cambridge, MA: Harvard University Press, 2009.

36. Arturo Escobar, *Territories of Difference: Place, Movement, Life, Redes*, Durham, NC: Duke University Press, 2008.

37. Federico Fuentes, "Government, Social Movements, and Bolivia Today,"

International Socialist Review 76 (March–April 2011); and the reply in the same issue by Jeffrey Webber, "Fantasies Aside, It's Reconstituted Neo-liberalism in Bolivia Under Morales."

38. Webber, "Fantasies Aside": 111.

39. Ibid., 48.

40. Lesley Gill, *Teetering on the Rim: Global Restructuring, Daily Life, and the Armed Retreat of the Bolivian State*, New York: Columbia University Press, 2000; Sian Lazar, *El Alto, Rebel City: Self and Citizenship in Andean Bolivia*, Durham, NC: Duke University Press, 2010.

41. What follows is a composite account based on Gill, *Teetering on the Rim*, and Lazar, *El Alto, Rebel City*.

42. Gill, *Teetering on the Rim*: 69.

43. Ibid.: 74–82.

44. Lazar, *El Alto, Rebel City*: 252–4. The theory of agonistic relations within social movements is elaborated in Chantal Mouffe, *On the Political*, London: Routledge, 2005.

45. Lazar, *El Alto, Rebel City*: 178. My emphasis.

46. Hardt and Negri, *Commonwealth*: 110.

47. Lazar, *El Alto, Rebel City*: 181, 258.

48. Ibid.: 178.

49. Ibid.: 180.

50. Ibid.: 260.

51. Ibid.: 63.

52. Ibid.: 34.

53. Murray Bookchin, *Remaking Society: Pathways to a Green Future*, Boston, MA: South End Press, 1990; "Libertarian Municipalism: An Overview," *Society and Nature* 1 (1992): 1–13; Elinor Ostrom, "Beyond Markets and Status: Polycentric Governance of Complex Economic Systems," *American Economic Review* 100 (2010): 641–72.

54. Hardt and Negri, *Commonwealth*.

55. Iris Marion Young, *Justice and the Politics of Difference*, Princeton, NJ: Princeton University Press, 1990.

Index